LETTS CREATIVE NEEDLECRAFTS

WHITEWORK

·JANE·DEW & VIV·WATKINS·

LETTS CREATIVE NEEDLECRAFTS

WHITEWORK

JANE DEW & VIV WATKINS

CHARLES LETTS · Letts · FOUNDED 1756

First published 1990
by Charles Letts & Company Ltd
Diary House, Borough Road
London SE1 1DW

Designed and produced by Rosemary Wilkinson
30 Blackroot Road, Sutton Coldfield, B74 2QP

Editor: Peta Abbott
Illustrator: Richard Draper
Designer: Patrick Knowles
Photographer: Pablo Keller

CIP catalogue record for this book is available from the British Library

ISBN 1 85238 106 X

Typeset by Fakenham Photosetting Ltd, Fakenham, Norfolk

Printed in Belgium

CONTENTS

Child's coat with heavy Broderie anglaise trimming on a white pique coat, c. 1910

DESIGN: PAST AND PRESENT

Religious and royal apparel, baby clothes and high fashion: all
have been enhanced with white embroidery during the long
history of this needlework.

Whitework is a general name covering many embroidery techniques, all of which use white thread on white fabric. There are some methods which are particularly associated with whitework and these rely on the use of texture and pattern contrasted with the basic fabric. The simple purity of whitework calls for a high standard of design and embroidery, which has been in evidence throughout its history.

The earliest whitework has been found in Coptic tombs, and it seems likely that such work was done in all parts of the Ancient world. Linen, which was the natural fibre available in Europe, was pulled and worked to give areas of regular patterns contrasted with areas of embroidery. The holes formed by the removal of warp and weft threads were overcast and filled with stitches. This developed into cutwork (reticello), the earliest needlemade lace.

Eventually, the fabric was discarded and the stitches were worked on a background of threads tacked onto parchment. This is known as punto in aria (stitches in the air). Much early whitework was produced for ecclesiastical use but, by the sixteenth century, Mary Queen of Scots had bed furnishings of darned net (lacis) and, during Mary's reign, the wearing of cutwork 'made beyond the sea' was forbidden to women below the rank of knight's wife.

The drawn thread work and punto in aria became very fashionable and were worked for ruffs (and later collars), ruffles, caps and aprons, as well as for household linen. However, surviving pieces tend to be items of special significance and quality, or samplers of techniques. By the seventeenth century, the samplers were of an extremely high standard and showed surface embroidery, as well as cutwork.

The fine quality linen thread produced in the Netherlands at the beginning of the eighteenth century encouraged the production of lighter and more diaphanous lace but this was very expensive. To curb extravagance, the duties on lace were very high and few people could afford even the smuggled laces. Cutwork was too heavy to replicate the delicate, flowing patterns and so a technique of pulled work developed, known as Dresden work. This method used a range of fine stitches to pull the warp and weft threads of fine cambric or imported Indian muslins.

Light gauzy cotton was also used for tambour work: a chain stitch worked on fabric held in a drum-like frame. The work quickly produced the decorated muslins so popular for the classical draped dresses of the period. British cottons, produced on the newly-patented machines at the end of the eighteenth century, became cheaper than those from India, and tambour workshops were set up which produced large quantities of commercial muslins. The method was also popular with ladies and muslin, ready-printed with designs, could be purchased to be worked at home.

The fine muslins went out of fashion after the Napoleonic Wars and a heavier weight muslin was used to make the collars, caps and baby clothes which came into style.

In 1814, Lady Mary Mongomerie of Eglinton Castle, Ayrshire, Scotland, brought back baby clothes from France which she showed to a Mrs Jamieson, who was already putting out the cotton from her husband's mills to be embroidered by outworkers. The satin stitch, eyelets, and patterns of delicate buttonhole and looped stitch filling in the cut-out spaces gave Ayrshire work a look of delicacy and fineness. The work was soon in

demand and was sold in other countries. However, the blockade on cotton exports imposed by the northern states in the American Civil War severely blighted the cotton industry and, although many areas recovered, the Swiss had produced a machine to imitate the work and Ayrshire could not compete. Some of the women earned a little producing broderie anglaise but this too could be done by machine. Several attempts were made to set up embroidery schools and

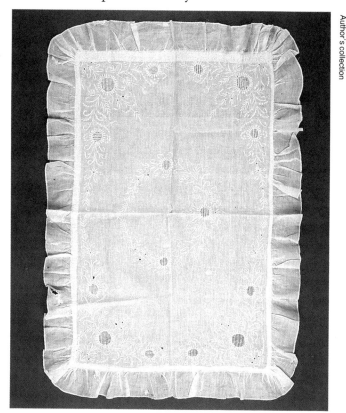

Author's collection

Lawn pillowcase embroidered with a variety of whitework stitches including eyelets and pulled work, c.1920

workshops to provide work during times of particular hardship; Mountmellick and Carrickmacross were styles of Irish whitework developed in this way. Ayrshire work was taken to Madeira after the phyloxera disease had killed the vines and ruined the wine industry, and this developed into what we now know as Madeira work.

Whenever whitework was in fashion the demand was very high and the same type of work was being produced not only in commercial sweatshops and by poorly paid outworkers but also in the home for personal use or for sale. Embroidery was considered a suitable occupation for women and was often the only respectable work available to a woman who had to earn her own living. Girls from the age of eight were employed in sweatshops where they were often overworked in appalling conditions. Home workers had a slightly better life but the work was poorly paid and late or imperfect work was not accepted. All the fashionable whitework techniques were available to ladies and some, such as tambour work, became a craze for a time. Much private work was of an extremely high standard but was considered to be 'women's work' and thus taken for granted.

By the end of the Victorian era, mass-produced, machine-made, whitework was widely available. Hand embroidery was seen as a leisure pastime and skilled work declined. As women's horizons broadened, they had less time for the detailed, time-consuming styles of embroidery and the working of such pieces became a labour of love.

Through the later half of the nineteenth century in England, Art Needlework was developing as a reaction against the flood of poorly-designed amateur work. William Morris and the Arts and Crafts Movement encouraged creative work, and Jessie Newbery at the Glasgow School of Art and Mrs Archibald Christie at the Royal College of Art were influential in raising the standards of technique and design. In the late nineteenth century in the Lake District of Britain, the writer and philanthropist, John Ruskin, encouraged the production of a style of cutwork, which was worked on and with linen threads in order to revive the traditional spinning and weaving of the area. The technique carries his name – Ruskin lace. It is also known as Greek lace because of the Greek-inspired reticella fillings which characterize the work. The Embroiderers' Guild was founded in 1904 to promote the standard of embroidery for amateur and professional alike. In 1945, the Needlework Development Scheme was extended 'to encourage greater interest in embroidery and to raise the standard of design' by expanding its collection of embroideries and its central reference library, and by extending its promotional work to art schools and other centres throughout the country.

In the twentieth century, experimental work using new techniques, such as machine embroidery, has opened up great possibilities for embroiderers. Appreciation of the past combined with an open-minded approach can result in original and satisfying work.

NEEDLES

The most vital piece of equipment for an embroiderer. Needles come in a range of thicknesses and lengths which are indicated by numbers: the highest number for the finest and shortest, and the lowest number for the thickest and longest of each type. Do store needles carefully in a needle case where the points will not be blunted or cause injury. Never use a rusty, distorted or blunt needle.

Always use the correct needle for the technique and the correct size for the work.

Betweens Short needles with a small round eye in a shaft of even thickness. Ideal for fast even stitching and for stitching fine fabrics. Sizes 1–10 (14s are occasionally available).

Crewel A long needle with a slim eye, ideal for working with crewel yarn and other threads of a similar construction, e.g. stranded cottons and silk. Sizes 2–10.

Sharps A medium length needle with a small eye, used for general sewing and tacking.

Tapestry Blunt needles with a large eye, designed to glide between the threads in counted thread work and needlepoint. Sizes 13–26.

PINS

Usually made in steel, a wide variety of pins are now available. Glass-headed pins are excellent reminders, brass pins are fine and ensure no rusty marks. Always store in a box and dispose of any rusty pins.

FABRICS

The range of fabrics encountered in shops is quite outstanding and a little daunting. The following is a brief guide to those fabrics essential to most embroidery and, in particular, the projects in this book.

COTTON

Calico An unbleached, coarse cotton, sold in its 'loomstate', i.e. before any treatment. Available in various weights and widths.

Lawn A fine, firm cotton woven from the finest, long, staple fibres.

Muslin A soft, semi-transparent cotton woven from fine but uneven fibres.

Organdie A stiff, transparent cotton woven from very fine fibres with a matt finish.

Poplin A firm, strong cotton woven from thicker fibres in a light twill weave with a slight sheen.

LINEN

This traditional strong fibre from Northern Europe produces a range of fabrics with excellent wearing and laundering characteristics. It is available in weights from the finest handkerchief linen to the thick, slubbed furnishing quality.

Even-weave A specialist fabric woven to a set number of threads per cm (in), varying from 36 to 11.

Hardanger A firm even-weave fabric with two threads woven as one and which is the proper fabric for Hardanger work, see page 16.

Cambric A fine glazed fabric particularly used for table linen and ecclesiastical vestments.

Handkerchief The finest linen, made especially for very fine work.

Linen is also combined with cotton, viscose and, occasionally, silk to make other fabrics. There are also good quality imitations of the linen fabrics but always check that the quality is adequate for the work to be undertaken.

NETS

Net is a sheer fabric woven so the threads form a hexagonal mesh. Net is woven in quite strong nylon, softer denier nylon, cotton and the finest of all, silk, known as tulle.

SILK

An exquisite fabric with a beautiful lustre which is spun by silk worms. Available in a vast range of weights and types from the finest tulles to the heavy slubbed tweeds. Silk has excellent draping qualities but needs careful laundering.

Organza A stiff, transparent silk woven from very fine fibres with a slight sheen.

THREADS

The third essential element for the embroiderer, forming the trio of fabric, needle and thread.

Coton à broder A single, non-stranded thread with a slight sheen. Excellent for pulled thread work.

Flower threads Manufactured in the Scandinavian countries. A fine, single-stranded, matt thread, of vegetable-dyed cotton with a wonderful lustre and a wide range of colours. Used for shadow work and broderie anglaise.

Crewel yarn A strong, 2-ply yarn, used for crewel embroidery, needlepoint and general embroidery.

Machine embroidery thread Specially spun to give a lustrous effect and not suitable for seams. Available in two thicknesses: 30s, fine, and 50s, slightly thicker.

Perlé Available in 2- or 3-ply, highly twisted, and offering a good range of thicknesses from No. 8 to No. 3 which is quite thick. Good for counted thread work.

Silk A growing range of products and colours are now available in this fibre, including stranded, twist and machine thread. Perfect for use with silk fabric and for general embroidery.

Soft embroidery cotton A matt, 5-ply, softly-twisted cotton which gives a solid colour. Good for solid lines and blocks in most techniques.

Stranded cotton and silk A universal thread of, usually, six strands which can be separated into any combination of strands.

OTHER EQUIPMENT

PAPER AND PENCILS

Used extensively at the design stage and for storage. Designs should always be worked on good quality paper but transferring can be worked from a more economical alternative, e.g. lining wallpaper.

Tissue is extremely useful for keeping work clean in a frame and for transferring designs. Acid-free tissue paper is ideal for embroidery and fabric storage.

Graph paper is used to show a design.

A good selection of hard (H) and soft (B) pencils is always useful.

SCISSORS

A pair of sharp, embroidery scissors, a pair of paper scissors and a pair of dressmaker's shears are all that are really required. Tailor's shears for heavy work and pinking shears for decorative, non-fray edges are useful but not essential.

STILETTO

A sharp-ended tool specifically designed to pierce holes in fabric. Essential for broderie anglaise, see page 44 but also useful for eyelet fastenings.

THIMBLE

A good quality thimble aids quick stitching and prevents punctured finger ends.

TRANSFER PENS AND PAPER

Water-soluble pens are ideal for tracing a design onto a fabric through which the design can be seen, e.g. organdie, organza, lawn or fine cotton. Iron-on pens are ideal for opaque fabrics but care must be taken to reverse the design. Available in 'one-off' and 'multiple' versions; both are water soluble on cotton. Do ensure that the tip of the pen is firm as a fuzzy line could distort a design.

Dry poster paint and a fine brush are also excellent, see page 86.

Iron-on pencils can be sharpened, thus a delicate line can be drawn.

Dressmaker's carbon is the original transfer medium. Never use typewriting carbon which leaves indelible marks.

FRAMES

With a few exceptions, e.g. net darning and patchwork, the majority of embroidery is more successful if worked in a frame. Large pieces of hand embroidery, including needlepoint, are almost invariably worked in a 'slate' frame.

Smaller pieces, or articles which have embroidery scattered in different areas, can be worked in the round, ring, hoop or 'tambour' frame. The tambour frame is named after a small Indian drum and, indeed, the framed fabric should be as tight as a drum. The frame consists of an inner ring and an outer ring with an adjustable screw bridging a split in the frame.

The tambour frame comes in a wide variety of diameters, from 7.5 cm (3 in) to 30 cm (12 in), usually made of plywood but occasionally in metal and plastic. A variety of models are now available, including table and floor stands, and clamps for chair arms or tables.

Hardanger is a counted thread embroidery and originates from the beautiful fjord area of western Norway. The combination of dominant cut-out areas, clusters of straight stitches, and delicate lace fillings and picots is characteristic of this method.

Fabric and threads

The fabric specific to Hardanger is made with two flat threads woven as one. All counted thread fabrics are available with a number of 'threads to the inch'. Hardanger fabric usually has 22 threads per inch (this is equivalent to 11 threads per inch canvas) and is traditionally in white or cream although pastel colours are also available. The stitching should always be worked in a matching thread.

The fabric has a matt texture and the threads used should complement this. Stranded cotton, coton à broder, matt threads and perlé are recommended but avoid very shiny 'floss' threads. The build up of geometric clusters in sympathetic threads produces remarkable effects, introducing an almost woven element to the fabric.

Method

As with all techniques which involve cutting away threads or areas of fabric, considerable care must be taken with the practical and visual impact of such removal. Practically, any removal must not weaken the overall area of the fabric. Visually, a void is created which needs balancing with rich surface stitching and lace-like stitches across the void. A combination of awareness of the design impact of the cut areas and the inherited traditions makes for rich and exciting work.

The cut areas are square or rectangular; the straight stitches, which are square, rectangular or chevron, are known as *kloster blocks*. Delicate lacy designs are introduced in the cut areas; simple looped stitches create *dove's eye* filling stitches and needleweaving creates *bars*. Picots can be formed on any of the edges (page 90).

The strong quality of Hardanger fabric and its simple stitching makes it a technique well suited to practical items. The fabric washes well.

Hardanger work is essentially a simple technique which depends on accuracy and care. A few basic steps will assist in the pursuit of this.

For small pieces, cut a piece of Hardanger the size of the finished article plus a border of several centimetres (an inch or two), and machine stitch or back stitch onto a piece of plain cotton. Place the cotton and the appliquéd fabric in a tambour or slate frame; tighten or string to achieve suitable tightness. Carefully, using the point of the scissors to lift the fabric, cut away the cotton to reveal the fabric underneath.

Always use a tapestry needle for any even-weave techniques as the blunt point glides between the threads easily; a sharp-pointed needle will pierce the threads. Weave in a few running stitches and then insert the needle where work is to commence, leaving a 'tail' of thread to be woven into the back of the work later (diagram 1). Knots detract from the quality of the work and are liable to come undone.

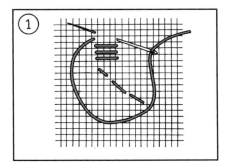

Using a contrasting coloured sewing thread, tack horizontal and vertical lines.

Work all the kloster blocks of the design surrounding the areas to be cut away. Use a satin stitch worked over identical numbers of thread (diagram 2).

Add extra decorative blocks and lines worked in satin stitch and back stitch (diagram 3).

Cut and draw threads in voided area. Cut the threads at the base of the kloster blocks and cut only threads running in the same direction as the satin stitches. Draw all the threads in one direction, then those in the other (diagram 4).

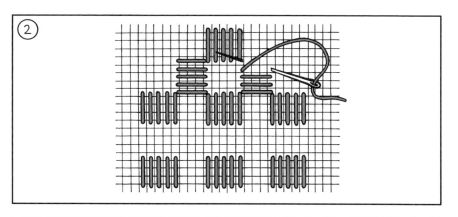

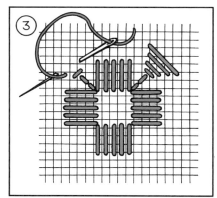

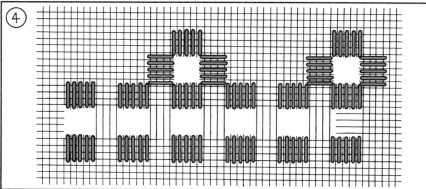

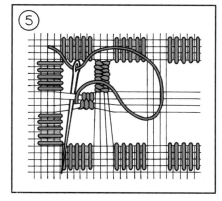

Work bars created by drawn threads by needleweaving with or without picots (diagrams 5 and 6).

Add lace filling stitches such as the single or extended dove's eye (diagrams 7 and 8).

Check back of work and ensure all thread ends are woven in through existing stitches.

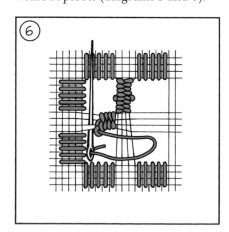

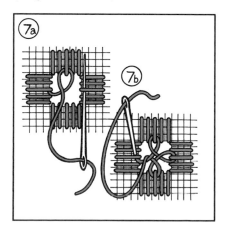

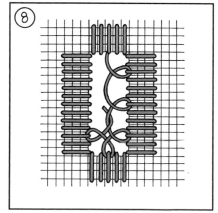

NAPKIN RING

Using a small repeat motif, the embroidery produces a very
decorative effect, which is totally practical. A lining of contrast
colour, perhaps to co-ordinate with existing table linen or china,
highlights the formal cut areas and is an
ideal vehicle for the stiffener.

A matt thread is advisable for an article which
will require fairly regular laundering; a 'shiny'
mercerized thread tends to lose its polish in
time. Do test the contrast fabric for colour
fastness; even the most reputable makes of
modern fabrics can have an unstable dye.
Washing the contrast fabric before making up
also ensures a 'pre-shrunk' fabric.

REQUIREMENTS

A small piece of white 22
    count Hardanger fabric
    18 cm (7 in) × 13 cm (5 in)
A skein of white coton à
    broder
A small piece of cotton fabric
    in a contrasting colour and
cut to the same size as the
    Hardanger fabric
Sufficient calico to dress a
    23 cm (9 in) tambour
    frame
Sewing thread to match the
    contrast cotton fabric
14 cm (5½ in) × 4.5 cm
    (1¾ in) of heavyweight
    fusible interfacing
Size 22 tapestry needle
Size 10 betweens needle for
    making up
A 23 cm (9 in) tambour
    frame

METHOD

WORKING THE EMBROIDERY

Take the piece of Hardanger fabric and frame up as directed in the skill file (page 16). Tack two parallel lines 2.25 cm (⅞ in) on either side of the longer centre tack line to indicate the edges and fold lines of the napkin ring. Tack another line 2 cm (¾ in) in from the left short side.

Refer back to the skill file (page 16) for details of the following steps. Following the chart on page 21 and starting at the lefthand tacked line, count two threads up from the centre tack line and work a kloster block of five vertical stitches over four threads, using coton à broder. Count four threads to the right and stitch a further 14 kloster blocks each separated by four threads and leaving two threads at the end. Count two threads down from the centre line and work a parallel row of kloster blocks facing the worked row. Above and below every third kloster block, work three more blocks, one vertical, two horizontal, over four threads.

Work the triangular blocks and back stitch details.

Carefully clip the threads for all the voids, withdrawing the threads for the middle row.

Needleweave the bars formed by the withdrawn threads in the middle row.

Work the dove's eye filling in the middle row and side blocks.

Check the back of the work and weave in all loose ends.

When all the motifs are complete, carefully remove the work and press gently, using steam and a little spray starch if needed.

MAKING UP

Cut a strip 4.5 cm (1¾ in) × 14 cm (5½ in) in heavyweight fusible interfacing. Cut a strip 13 cm (5 in) × 18 cm (7 in) in pre-shrunk contrast cotton and iron the interfacing to the wrong side of this, allowing 2 cm (¾ in) seam allowance along the sides and the long edge (diagram 1).

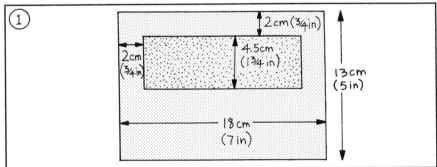

Form into a ring with a seam 2 cm (¾ in) wide at the short ends, trim the corners and press the seam open (diagram 3).

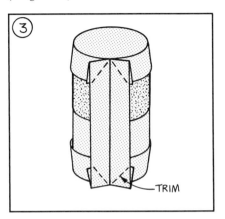

Carefully press a 2 cm (¾ in) turning on both long edges (diagram 2).

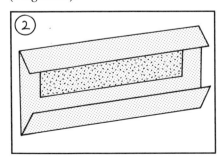

Press the ring in half along the edge of the interfacing and slip stitch the two edges together (diagram 4).

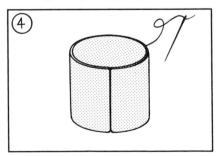

Fray several threads from the spare Hardanger, or use an exact match in linen thread. Place the two short edges of the Hardanger together (wrong sides facing) and pin so that there are two free vertical threads on either side of the embroidery. Stitch the seam, using a small back stitch over two threads at a time. Press the seam open. Press a turning down on one long side (diagram 5).

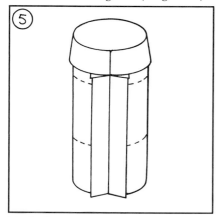

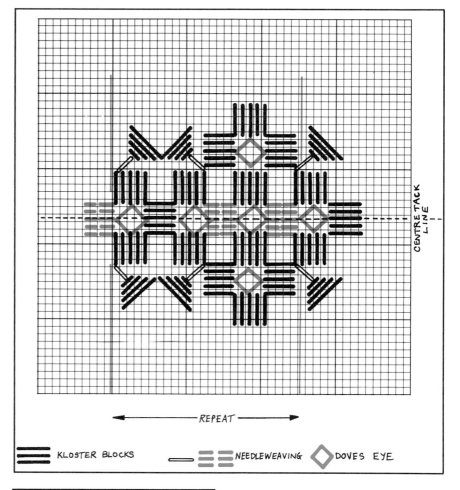

CENTRE TACK LINE

←———— REPEAT ————→

▬▬▬▬ KLOSTER BLOCKS   ══ ══ NEEDLEWEAVING   ◇ DOVES EYE

Tack the contrast cotton ring onto the Hardanger ring ensuring that the edge of the cotton ring matches exactly along the edge tacking (diagram 6).

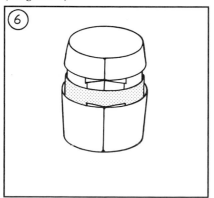

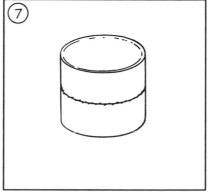

Fold the Hardanger fabric over the contrast ring, tack the folded edge over the raw edge and carefully slip stitch every two or three threads (diagram 7).

When all the stitching is complete, turn the ring right side out. The edges can be finished with buttonhole stitch four threads deep, further embellished with picots or left plain.

CUSHION

The hardwearing character of Hardanger work makes it an ideal candidate for soft furnishings. Although not intended for situations where hard wear or soiling would occur, i.e. a child's room or a kitchen, the embroidery would certainly withstand many years' wear as a scatter cushion in a sitting room.

The cut areas of the technique look particularly effective when placed over a contrasting colour. The contrast can be effective in a small area, as with the napkin ring, or, in larger areas, as shown on the cushion. The life of the cushion will undoubtedly be longer than any colour scheme in a room and the contrast colour could easily be changed to co-ordinate with a new colour scheme.

REQUIREMENTS

75 cm (30 in) of white 22 count Hardanger fabric, 110 cm (43 in) wide
4 skeins of white No. 5 perlé cotton per side
1 metre (1 yard) cotton fabric in a contrasting colour to make the undercover and bias cut strips for piping (optional)
Purchased cushion pad 45 × 45 cm (18 × 18 in)
Sewing thread to match the Hardanger and contrasting cotton fabric
Size 22 tapestry needle
Size 10 betweens needle for making up
A 23 cm (9 in) tambour frame

WORKING THE EMBROIDERY

Cut two pieces of Hardanger fabric 50 cm (20 in) square and neaten the edges with either oversewing or machine zigzag stitch to prevent fraying.

With tacking stitch in a contrasting coloured sewing thread, mark the vertical and horizontal centre lines. Also tack lines 2.5 cm (1 in) in from the four edges as position guides for the corner motifs (diagram 1).

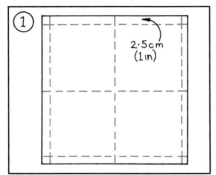

Place in the frame. Starting at the exact centre hole created by the weave of the fabric, count 42 threads along one tacked line and stitch the first diagonal row of kloster blocks as shown on the chart, using the perlé (diagram 2).

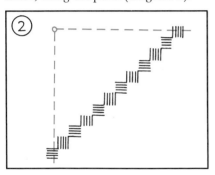

Repeat the sequence in the other three quarters, turning the work so that the first kloster block is always the same (diagram 3).

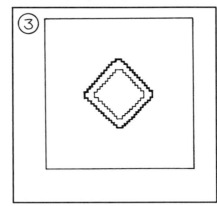

Work all the kloster blocks that surround the areas to be cut and withdrawn.

Withdraw and cut all the threads as shown on the chart.

Work the woven bars.

Stitch all the dove's eye fillings.

Repeat the triangular motif in each corner, with the centre hole exactly in the corner of the tacked lines and the withdrawn threads and needleweaving at the side edges replaced by kloster blocks over two threads.

Work the second side in exactly the same way or, leave it unembroidered but mark the two centre lines.

MAKING UP

Press the work from the wrong side but leave the tacking lines in

position to help match sides.

Tack the two sides, right sides together, taking great care that, if both sides are embroidered, the pattern is exactly matched. To do this, pin along the two centre tacking lines, then match the four corners. A perfect effect can be achieved if a thread is pulled out at exactly the position of the tacking for the seams. The tacking can then be worked along this line through the two thicknesses of linen. Piping can be added at this stage, see general skill file (page 89).

Machine stitch along the tacking line, taking care to keep within the pulled thread line. Stitch three sides and 4 cm (2½ in) in from both corners along the fourth side (diagram 4).

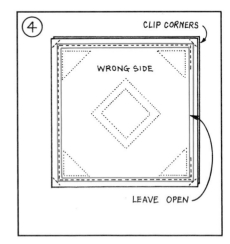

Clip the corners carefully.

Turn right side out and press the stitched edges gently; a hot iron and too much pressure will result in a shiny surface. Press in the seam allowance along the pulled thread lines of the two sides of the opening.

The cushion cover can now be trimmed to suit the worker's taste but do avoid trimmings that will overwhelm the intricate embroidery. A cord made to match the linen and the backing fabric would complement the embroidery. Tassels made in white or the contrast colour would also enhance the work (see skills file on page 89).

Make up the undercover in the contrasting fabric in the same way as the embroidered cover.

Place the cushion pad inside the undercover, then, using a matching sewing thread, neatly stitch the two edges of the opening together. Place inside the embroidered cover and stitch up the opening as before. This can then be unpicked when the cover needs laundering (diagram 5).

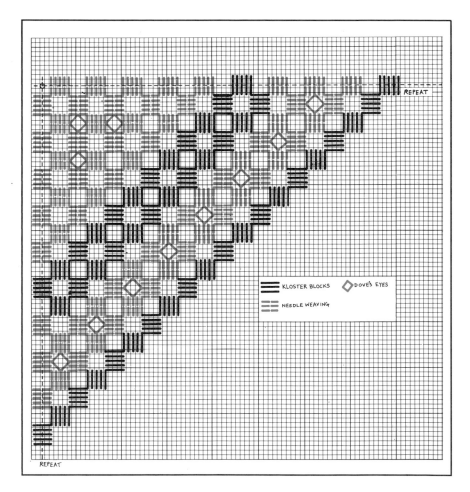

REPEAT

KLOSTER BLOCKS   DOVE'S EYES

NEEDLE WEAVING

REPEAT

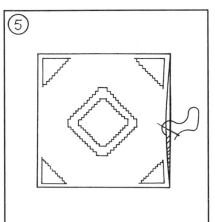

⑤

ROLLER BLIND

Openwork techniques are effective mounted over a contrast colour which will show through, as in the napkin ring, or where light can shine through. Lampshades, window decals and curtains are all excellent uses for Hardanger work.

The formal, lattice effect of Hardanger work lends itself to any design with an architectural basis. Most architectural styles could provide inspiration but Northern European buildings seem to have the most direct relationship to Hardanger; tall Dutch houses, the broader buildings of the Hanseatic League countries, the wooden houses of Norway, are all ideal.

The design used for the roller blind comes from an area of Edinburgh where the architecture combines height, formality and decorative elements. The void or openwork areas are used for the windows in the design but equal emphasis is given to the blocks of stitchery which form the roofs, walls and decorative features.

REQUIREMENTS

Sufficient 22 count Hardanger fabric for the chosen window, remembering that the widest Hardanger fabric is 170 cm (67 in), in white, beige or cream
A selection of perlé cotton, coton à broder, and

stranded cotton to match the fabric
Sewing thread to match the fabric
A can of roller blind stiffener
Roller blind kit to fit the chosen window
Size 22 tapestry needle

Size 10 betweens needle for making up
A 23 cm (9 in) tambour frame
Staple gun or tacks to attach embroidered fabric to roller blind

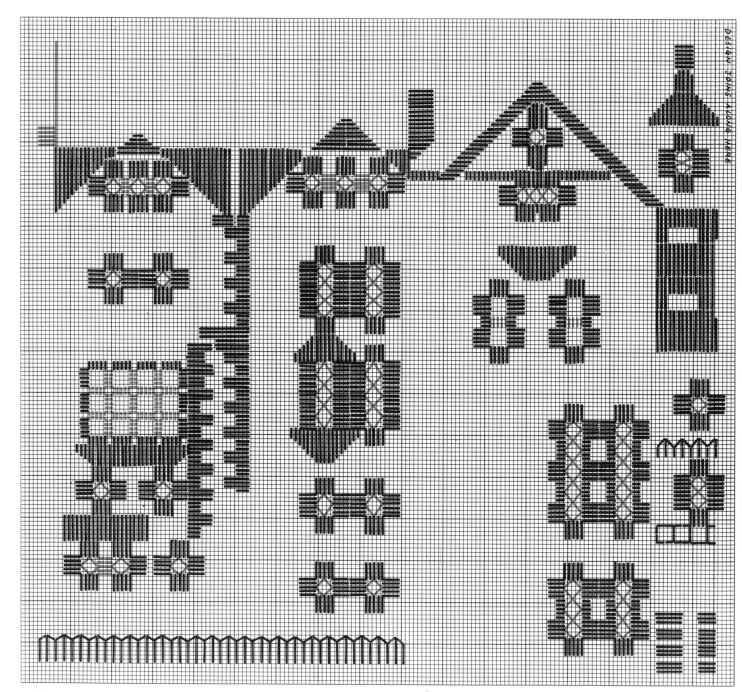

DESIGN JOINS ALONG HERE

KLOSTER BLOCKS ⎯⎯ BACK STITCH ≣≣ NEEDLEWEAVING ◇ DOVES EYE

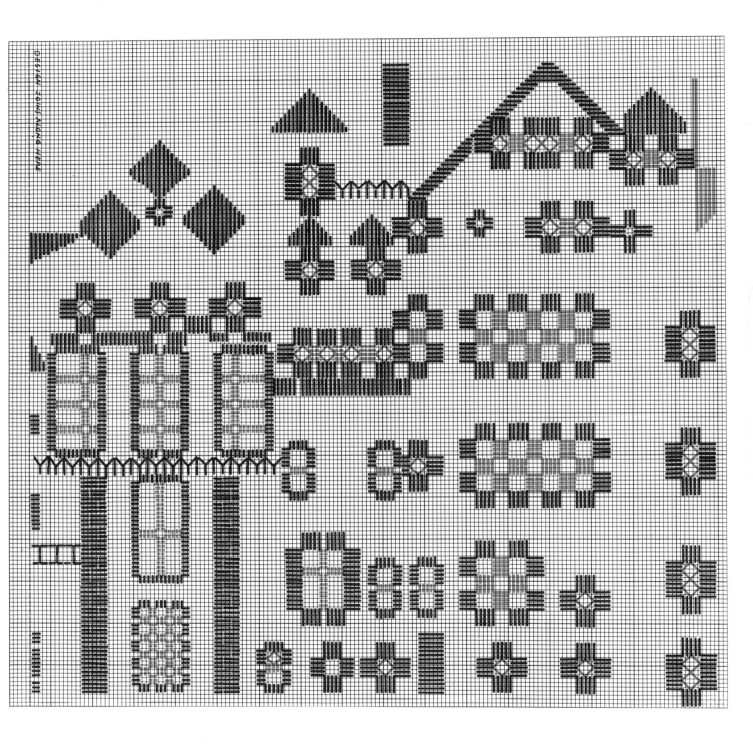

WORKING THE EMBROIDERY

Cut a piece of Hardanger fabric the exact width of the window plus 2.5 cm (1 in) turnings each side and the length of the window plus 15 cm (6 in). Roll one end up tightly with tissue paper rolled inside and loosely tack over the roll, leaving at least 30 cm (12 in) for the design. Using a contrasting thread, tack a centre vertical line and a line 10 cm (4 in) up from the edge, to indicate the bottom of the design. Place in the frame (diagram 1).

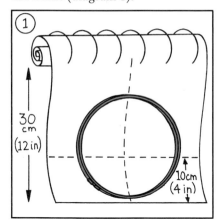

Starting with the centre line marked on the chart on pages 28, 29, stitch the kloster blocks around all the 'windows', using perlé cotton.

Stitch all the kloster blocks which form 'brick' details or 'roof' shapes.

Carefully clip all the threads in the 'window' areas and needleweave all the remaining bars, using coton à broder.

Work dove's eye filling for 'curtain' details in perlé cotton.

Work back stitch for 'balconies' and architectural details in three strands of cotton.

Once the whole design has been worked, repeat the whole design, or part of the design, to fill as much of the roller blind as is desired.

MAKING UP

Carefully press on the wrong side. Hem the sides with plain back stitch or by withdrawing two vertical threads and working a decorative hem stitch (diagram 2). Use a pulled thread or matching linen thread. Following the manufacturer's instructions, make a hem deep enough to take the batten which keeps the blind rigid. Hem as for

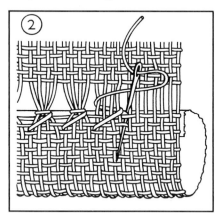

the sides, leaving an opening along the base hem to allow insertion of the batten (diagrams 3 and 4). Attach the fabric to the roller blind unit according to the manufacturer's instructions and use the stiffening agent.

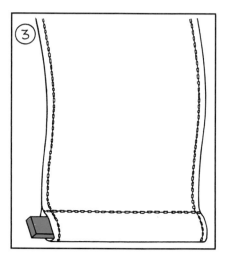

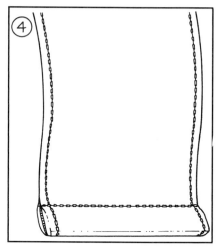

The cord and 'acorn' to pull and release the blind must be carefully chosen to enhance the delicate lattice work of the embroidery. The one provided by the manufacturer may be suitable or could be replaced by a cord and tassel made from a selection of embroidery threads (refer to skill file on page 88), or by a cord and large wooden, china or glass bead.

EXPERIMENTING

The formal filigree effect of Hardanger is well suited to tablelinen and the design for the napkin ring could be repeated all round, or worked in separate motifs, on a tablecloth or place mats.

The affinity of the technique with architecture gives a wonderful source of inspiration. Look at the Netherlands, Amsterdam in particular, and Georgian buildings for further ideas.

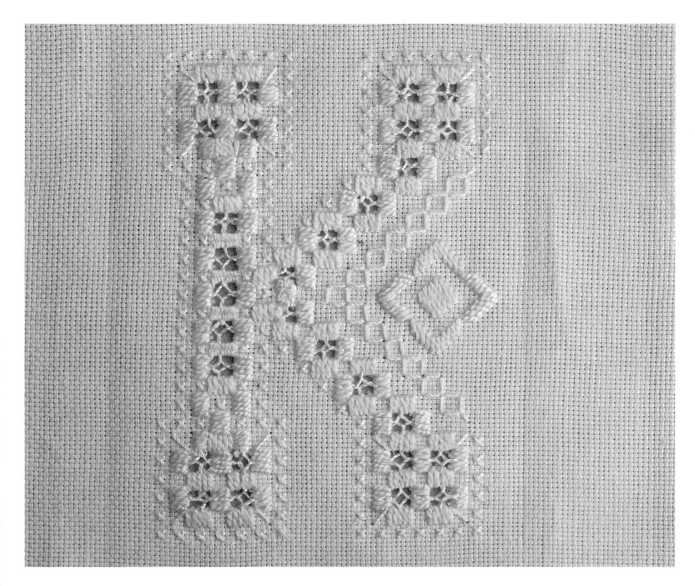

Using Hardanger to embellish the geometric form of a letter of the alphabet

CUTWORK

A wonderful technique whose name evokes thoughts of crisp table linen and delicate summer clothes. Cutwork is popular for napkins, pillowcases, children's and women's clothes, and ecclesiastical embroidery, and the technique for such items offers the ideal combination of effective decorative qualities and excellent laundering characteristics.

Cutwork has a long history, with many variations from all over Europe. As with most embroidery methods, an awareness of traditional design always helps the designer and worker when creating a new piece of work. Traditional designs invariably evolve by trial and error, so it is well worth studying the proportions and stitchery of such pieces. In a similar manner to Hardanger work, all the national cutwork techniques have a common basis of a balance between the strong voided areas and the filigree effects of the embroidered bars, picots and needleweaving.

In the most simple forms of cutwork, the cut areas are quite small but, when strengthening bars are introduced, the cut areas can be much larger. The scale of the cut areas is governed by the weave of the fabric and the area to be decorated. A fine cotton lawn will not support a very large and ornate cutwork area and equally, a large linen tablecloth requires a bold design to carry rich detail around and across the cut areas.

Much of the delight in cutwork relies on the relationship between the shape of the cut areas, the fabric and the even quality of the stitching. In its most complicated form – the technique *reticella* where the fillings in the cut area are worked in buttonhole stitch – it is almost indistinguishable from lace.

Fabrics and threads

It is a technique which requires a considerable investment in skill and time, so it is important to ensure that the choice of design, fabric, thread and purpose all reflect that investment.

Traditionally, cutwork is worked on firm linen or cotton but in reality, any non-fraying, close-woven fabric may be used, ranging from fine organdie to a heavier woollen fabric. In most cases, coton à broder is an ideal thread but stranded cotton, perlé, or even crewel, persian or tapestry yarn can be used to great effect. The stitching should be carried out with betweens or crewel needles.

Careful laundering and cleaning is always recommended for all embroidered work but cutwork responds well and the potential heirloom will, with care, last for many generations.

Method

All the cutwork techniques have a common basic procedure, and care taken at this stage will be well rewarded when the work is complete. Once the design is transferred onto the fabric, a fine running stitch is 'drawn' along it. This stitching serves two purposes: to increase the clarity of the design and to strengthen the edge of the cut areas. Stitching should always start by tacking a few stitches towards the beginning of the embroidery. This 'tail' is unthreaded after the embroidery is worked and rethreaded through the back of the stitches. To finish, weave the thread into the back of previous stitching.

Outline the transferred design with a fine running stitch in coton à broder or perlé (diagram 1).

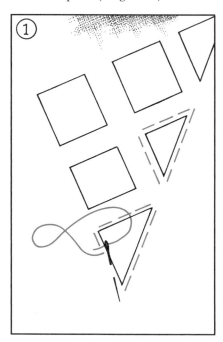

To create the bars, take threads across the area to be cut away. The exact number of threads is dependent on the size of the cut away area. Work a fine, even buttonhole stitch over the threads, ensuring that the fabric underneath is not caught by the needle. (The insertion of a clean cocktail stick or toothpick can be useful to lift the threads away from the fabric, but care must be taken that the threads are not stretched as you work them, so that the bar will not lie flat.) See diagrams 2 and 3.

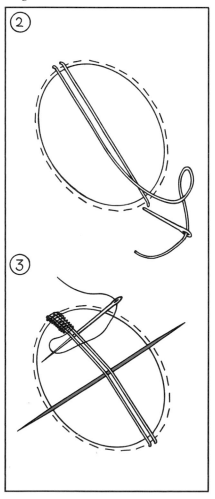

Work a fine, even buttonhole stitch over all the lines of the running stitch, outlining the areas to be cut and working from left to right (diagram 4). The 'ridge' of the stitch should lie against the area to be cut away. Tailor's buttonhole stitch may also be used (page 90). The stitches should all lie at right angles to the outline, except where there is a point or a corner in the design. In

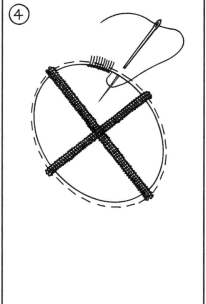

such cases, the stitches must be spaced out or extended to accommodate the shape.

When all the bars and outlines have been embroidered, the fabric can be cut away. This must be carried out with a very sharp, fine pair of embroidery scissors. Pierce the centre of the area to be cut away and work towards the buttonholed

edge. Clip as closely to the buttonholed edge as is possible and take great care not to cut any of the edge stitches or bars (diagram 5).

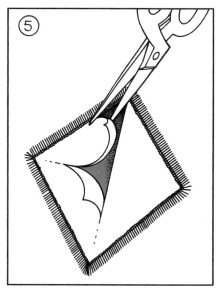

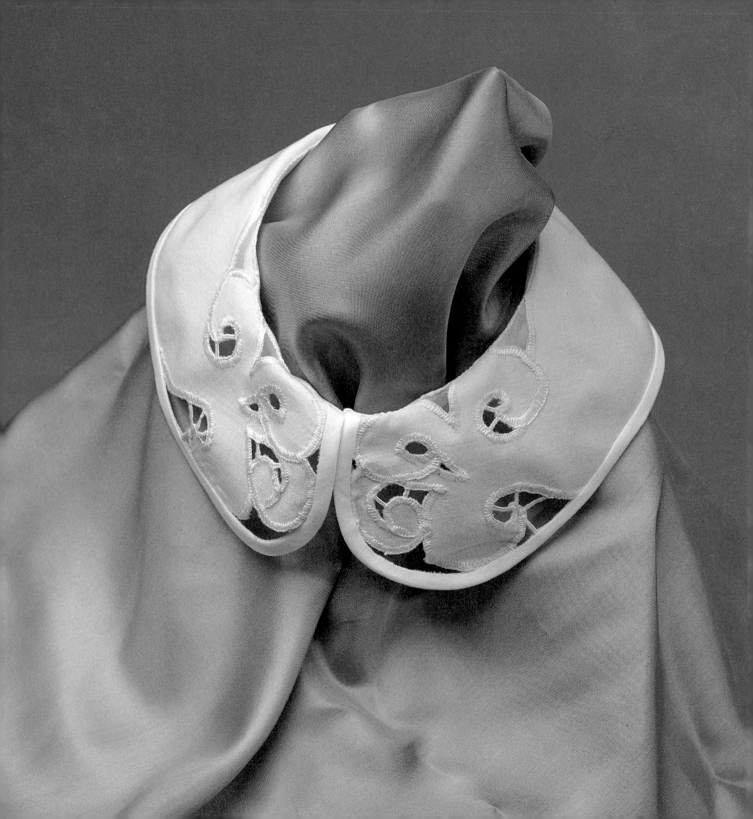

COLLAR

Throughout all eras of fashion there has always been a place for a decorative collar. The size of the collar and the degree of decoration has varied tremendously but cutwork has always been in evidence.

In recent years, there has been a great resurgence of interest and pleasure taken in fashion embroidery and not just for glamorous evening wear. Many of the fashion designers regularly use embroidery in their collections and a round collar is the perfect partner for many garments. Richly-patterned woollen knitwear, delicate, knitted cottons, formal tailored suits, romantic summer dresses, T-shirts, and plain blouses and shirts are all ideal vehicles for an ornately decorated collar, such as the design given here.

This is a skilled piece for an experienced embroiderer.

REQUIREMENTS

Commercial collar pattern
Sufficient fine white cotton
  lawn or poplin to make
  collar (check with
  commercial pattern first)
White sewing thread

1 skein of white coton à
  broder
Purchased decorative bias
  binding or sufficient
  matching fabric to make
  bias strips

Size 10 betweens needle
A 23 cm (9 in) tambour
  frame
A sheet of plain paper
Transfer pen or alternative

Preparation

Using a commercial pattern of a suitable size, mark the outline of the pattern piece for the collar onto the fabric to be embroidered, and indicate the stitching lines with a line of tacking. With a water-soluble pen, make a mark 5 cm (2 in) in from either side of the front edge as shown on the motif on page 37. With a ruler, make a line from the corners of the collar to the marks and indicate the lines with tacking stitches (diagram 1).

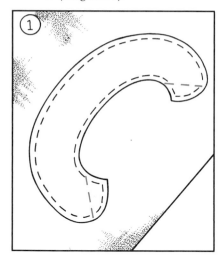

Place the fabric to be embroidered over the design matching up the diagonal line exactly and transfer with tinted white poster paint or a water-soluble pen (page 86). Place the fabric in a dressed embroidery frame as shown in the skill file (page 86).

Working the embroidery

More details of the cutwork technique are shown in the skill file on pages 32 and 33.

Stitch the outline of the design with a small running stitch.

Work all the bars in the design.

Stitch in buttonhole stitch around all the areas to be cut and the extra design lines.

Carefully cut away all the areas of fabric to be removed inside the

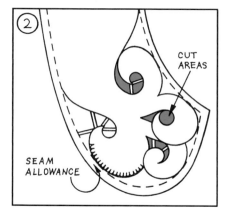

collar, taking extra care where there are worked bars (diagram 2).

Making up

Machine stitch along the tacked seam lines to form 'stay' stitches to prevent stretching. Carefully cut out the collar, allowing a 1 cm (½ in) seam allowance outside the machine-stitched line. The outer edge of the collar can be bound with a bias strip cut from the same fabric as the collar, or use a fine commercial bias binding (diagram 3). Some of the commercial bindings are decorative and a careful

choice could add to the delicate quality of the collar. The inside collar edge should be bound with a 5 cm (2 in) deep bias binding cut from the collar fabric or similar to

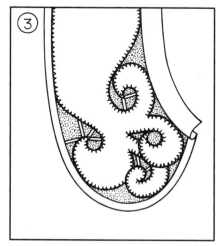

allow the collar to be tacked inside a garment. Cut away the remaining areas carefully (diagram 4).

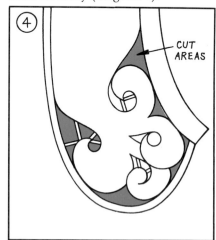

The collar should be laundered frequently and weak starch will help to retain the original freshness.

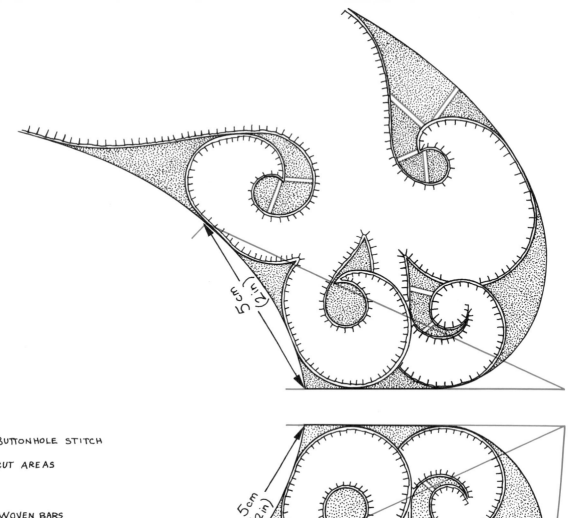

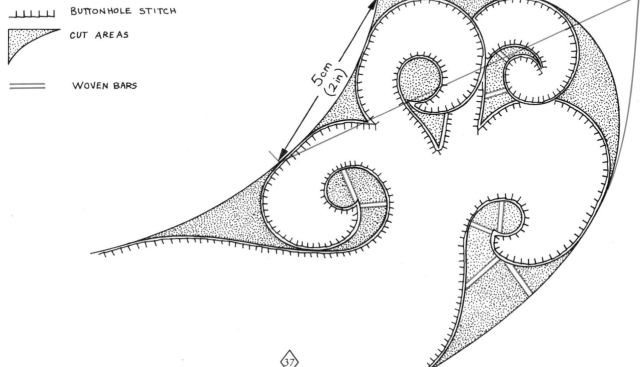

┴┴┴┴┴ BUTTONHOLE STITCH

CUT AREAS

WOVEN BARS

5 cm (2 in)

5 cm (2 in)

LAMPSHADE

Choose a commercial, conical or 'coolie' shade covered
with a soft cotton fabric in a colour to complement the room
where the shade is to be used. The additional embroidered
fabric to be placed over the shade will reduce the amount of
light and this should be considered when choosing the colour
of the shade.

The use of cutwork for a lampshade offers two very different effects. When the light is switched off, the cutwork looks most ornamental with the colour of the shade showing through the cut areas. When the light is switched on, two variations of the shade colour are created: one, undiluted, showing through the embroidery, the other a paler version where the white fabric lies over the shade, creating a delicate lace-like effect.

Always use the wattage of bulb recommended for the commercial shade.

REQUIREMENTS

Purchased 'coolie'
  lampshade covered in
  plain cotton in chosen
  colour
Sufficient white cotton poplin
  fabric to cover the shade,
  see below

1 skein of white coton à
  broder or 1 skein of white
  No. 8 perlé cotton
Purchased binding or
  sufficient poplin to make a
  bias binding wide enough
  to cover the wired edges
  of the shade

Size 10 betweens needle
A 23 cm (9 in) tambour
  frame
Several sheets of plain
  paper
Transfer pens or alternative
White sewing thread

MEASURING UP

Using a large sheet of paper and masking tape, which does not leave any residue, cover the entire shade. Mark the upper and lower edges and the line of the seam. Remove the paper carefully, cut along the seam lines and upper and lower edges, then place on a flat surface; this now forms the pattern for the embroidered shade. Divide the upper and lower edge lines into equal sections, i.e. first halves, then quarters, eighths and sixteenths, and mark. Join the upper and lower

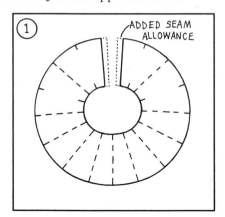

marks (diagram 1) across the pattern to create sections large enough to contain the design 16 × 11.5 cm (6¼ × 4½ in), see page 42. Draw the design in each section using the centre lines of the design and avoiding the seam lines (diagram 2).

Carefully measure the total area of the lampshade pattern and check that it will fit onto a standard width fabric, i.e. 90 cm (36 in), 120 cm (45 in). If the total area is too large,

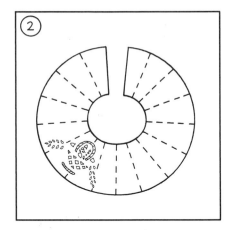

the shade will have to be made in two parts (a very large shade may need four) with another seam exactly opposite the existing seam. Lay the pattern pieces on an imaginary length of fabric, 90 cm (36 in) or 120 cm (45 in) wide, so that the centre line of each pattern piece is at 90° to the imaginary grain line (i.e. to the selvage) and there is a seam allowance of 1 cm (½ in), see diagram 3. The required length of

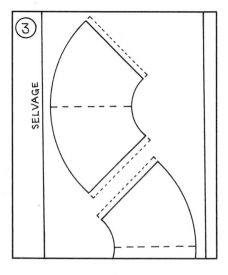

fabric can now be assessed. This apparently complicated procedure allows for a totally free choice of lampshade size and can be adapted to accommodate a shade suitable for a small side lamp or a large, central room light.

Place the pattern pieces on the fabric, ensuring that the centre lines are at 90° to the selvage. Transfer the seam allowance and centre line markings.

Place the embroidery design under a fabric piece matching the centre lines. Transfer the design onto the fabric with tinted, dry poster paint and a fine brush, or with a water-soluble pen. Repeat the transfer procedure on all the pieces.

Place one piece of the fabric into a tambour frame as described in the skill file (page 86). As the stitching in cutwork is quite dense, the sewing thread can become quite worn, so it is important to work with a slightly shorter thread than usual.

WORKING THE EMBROIDERY

For more details of the cutwork technique, look back at the skill file on pages 32 and 33.

Work running stitches around the leaf, petal and other areas to be cut.

Work all the bars on the leaves and handle.

Stitch with buttonhole stitch around all the areas to be cut.

Carefully cut away all the fabric to be removed.

Repeat the procedure with all the pieces.

When all the embroidery is completed, mark the seam lines with tacking. Carefully wash the work if needed, pinning it out as shown in the skill file (page 86). If the work is washed, a very weak solution of traditional starch could be used; if not, the work could be gently sprayed with an 'instant' starch. This helps the fabric to maintain its crispness while the seams are being stitched and the embroidered shade is being stitched onto the purchased shade. Press gently on the wrong side of the work using a damp cloth to remove any creases.

MAKING UP

Cut out the separate pieces and handle carefully as the bias cut edges may stretch. If stretching does occur, gentle pressing with a damp cloth will remove most of the stretching.

With the wrong sides together and using brass pins, pin and tack the fabric pieces together.

When all the pieces are tacked together, place the cover gently over the shade, right side uppermost, taking care not to stretch the upper and lower edges, which are bias cut (diagram 4). Check that the embroidered shade fits the purchased shade well, but allow for

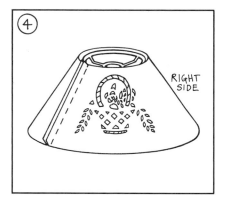

a little ease as the French seams used to enclose any raw edges will take up this. See page 87. Adjust the tacked seams if necessary.

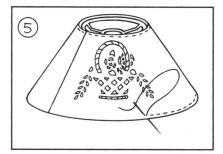

Once the fit is acceptable, remove the embroidered shade gently and stitch the seams, by hand or machine, using a small stitch 6 mm (¼ in) outside the tacked line.

Clip the raw edges very carefully and unpick the tacking. Turn to wrong side and pin along needle holes for the tacking, enclosing the first seam and raw edges. Stitch the second seam to form the French seam. Press the seams, all in the same direction.

Place the embroidered shade carefully over the purchased shade,

matching upper and lower edges and catching the two shades together with brass pins. (Small pieces of double-sided tape could be used at this stage to hold the fabric in position on the shade but it should not be relied on as a permanent means of attachment.) Using a fine betweens needle and white sewing thread, attach the embroidery to the shade with a fine stab stitch just inside the wire frame at top and bottom (diagram 5).

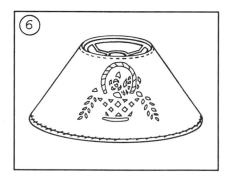

Once the embroidery is securely stitched to the shade, a finish is needed for the upper and lower edges. A white or co-ordinating colour in bias-cut fabric is the ideal finish; a bias binding is essential to accommodate the curves. A highly decorated edge would detract from the embroidery (diagram 6).

If the embroidered part of the lampshade needs cleaning, the fabric can be removed, washed and restitched fairly easily but it would be advisable to 'stay' stitch the upper and lower edges to prevent stretching. Give a gentle hand wash and add a little weak starch.

CUT AREAS

WOVEN BARS

CENTRE LINE

EXPERIMENTING

Cutwork offers curves and flowing lines as a perfect complement to the formal lines of Hardanger. Its cut areas have a great similarity to stencil designs and the resurgence of interest in the art of stencilling gives the cutwork embroiderer an endless source of designs.

The remarkable practicality of a technique which looks so fragile makes it suitable for all sorts of items. Work designs in different scales on shirts, nightdresses, table linen, children's clothes, bedlinen, cushions and even curtains. Traditionally worked on fine cotton, cutwork is also successful on closely woven wool and even denim. Adjust the scale of the design and the thickness of the thread to suit the fabric. Always work cutwork in a thread to match the fabric; coloured stitchery detracts from the richness of the technique.

This crisp white collar provides a rich example of the possibilities of producing cutwork by sewing machine

43

Broderie anglaise is probably one of the most easily recognized forms of embroidery and is used in its strip form to decorate all types of clothing, tablelinen and bedlinen. Apart from lace, it is certainly the most popular choice in commercially available trimmings and, like lace, can be produced industrially or by hand.

It has a wealth of small but simple detail based around eyelets, or tiny cut areas, of different shapes. Although similar to cutwork, broderie anglaise does not have any stitches across the cut areas apart from ladder stitches across linear shapes. A rich variety of surface stitches – satin, stem, chain and buttonhole stitch, and French knots (page 90) – are used to decorate the fabric around the eyelets and produce a dainty effect.

Fabrics and threads

Broderie anglaise is traditionally produced on a fine linen or cotton which reflects its origins in Czechoslovakian folk embroidery. An awareness of that tradition helps the contemporary worker to select a fabric which will also be successful. Lawn, fine flannel, crêpe de Chine, cambric, muslin and a firm silk are all good choices. The thread should match the fabric choice in weight, colour and texture. Coton à broder, stranded cotton, perlé, matt linen, matt flower cotton, or silk twist all work well. Two strands of cotton on fine lawn is a good indicator.

Equipment

The smallest eyelets are made by piercing the fabric with a stiletto. This item was often richly decorated with a mother-of-pearl handle and antique stilettos can occasionally be found in old sewing boxes and at antique sales. In the past, eyelets would have been made to carry ribbon and tape to fasten underwear and infant's clothes. Stilettos are still available today and, if an antique one is to be used, clean it very thoroughly first with fine emery paper to remove any trace of rust from the shaft, which is usually made of steel.

Betweens and sharps needles carry thread smoothly and will assist in even stitching. Extremely sharp, fine-pointed embroidery scissors are essential to cut out the tiny areas in broderie anglaise. The work is always carried out in a tambour frame to ensure even stitching.

Broderie anglaise produces a delightfully fresh-looking effect and much of this charm lies in keeping the work clean. Do use new, rust-free needles and keep the lengths of embroidery thread fairly short to avoid the soiling that can occur when the threads are long. Take a little time to study the design as there are several stages with broderie anglaise and it is at its most successful if each stage is completed before the next is started.

Method

Start all the work with a few tiny back stitches in an area to be covered with embroidery and finish off by threading through the back of previous stitching. Only carry thread from one motif to another if the distance between is tiny.

Work on the smallest holes first by running a small stab stitch (page 91) around the shape. This both strengthens the hole to be pierced and pads the overcasting (diagram 1).

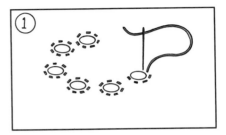

When the stab stitches are complete, pierce the centre of each small hole with the sharp point of the stiletto (diagram 2).

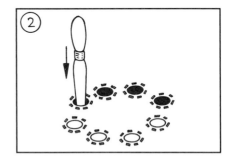

Next work the overcasting, ensuring that the stitches are even in depth and lie together neatly (diagram 3). It is well worth practising a little first to achieve a good tension for the overcasting.

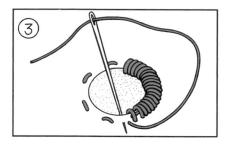

Make stab or running stitches around the larger shapes. When the running stitches are complete, pierce the centre of each shape with sharp embroidery scissors, then make small cuts from the centre out

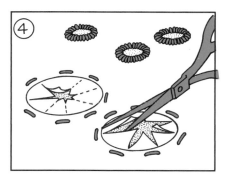

to the stitching (diagram 4). Turn the little fabric flaps to the back of the work and overcast round as before. The overcasting will catch the flaps down. Clip away any remaining flaps (diagram 5).

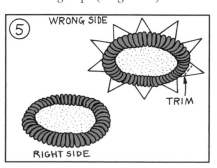

Follow this sequence of outline stitching and clipping with the other shapes. These may include petal or 'daisy', triangle, oval and 'cucumber seed' shapes (diagram 6).

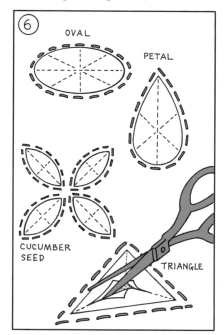

The shapes may be 'shaded' by introducing some running stitches for padding at the base of a shape and elongating the overcasting in this area (diagram 7).

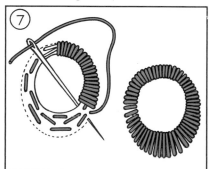

Some of the shapes can be linked up to form repeat patterns. In this case, work the running stitches in a wave pattern, so that the shapes are joined with thread for strength (diagram 8); follow the same sequence for overcasting.

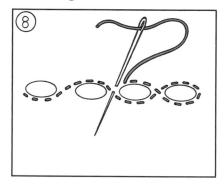

Large uncut shapes are worked in padded satin stitch. Work a row of satin stitches inside the shape with

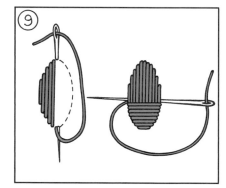

the stitches at right angles to the finished stitching (diagram 9). Work the second row of satin stitch exactly on the transferred line to cover the padding. Work all the smaller shapes with French knots. Use split or stem stitch for thin lines and chain stitch for thicker lines.

CHRISTENING GOWN

Christening gowns and, perhaps, samplers are tailor-made heirlooms. Space is often left in the first working of such pieces for the addition of other names, initials or dates. White is always used for the gowns and whitework techniques have been used for some exquisite gowns.

Broderie anglaise is a perfect technique for a gown as its traditional formality in design and excellent laundering qualities accommodate further additions and the reappearance of the gown at future celebrations. The selection of good quality fabric is essential and a pure cotton is recommended. Cotton will last well over the years and will stand fairly rigorous washing if accidents happen. Depending on the season of the year, a fine lawn or poplin is a good choice. A soft wool could be used but careful laundering and storage are essential.

The choice of garment for a christening is wide as long as it has a separate yoke. The embroidered yoke could also be part of a sleeveless summer gown with a short skirt, a puff-sleeved, longer gown or a neat smock to be worn with shorts. The choice of garment is entirely individual, requiring only a square or round yoke with a centre back opening.

REQUIREMENTS

Commercial pattern, see below
Sufficient white lawn for the whole garment (check with commercial pattern first)

2 skeins of white stranded cotton
White sewing thread
Size 10 sharps or betweens needle
A 23 cm (9 in) tambour frame

A large sheet of plain paper
Pencils, smudge-proof black felt-tip pen
White and coloured poster paint and a fine brush
Stiletto

WORKING THE EMBROIDERY

Select a commercial pattern for the size of the child when he or she is to be christened. It is advisable to be generous with the size; a gown which is too big is at least wearable which is not the case if the gown is too small. Babies can grow very fast, so do allow for growth when choosing the size.

Trace the pattern for the yoke onto a sheet of plain paper and show seam allowances, etc. Mark the centre front very clearly and mark a line 4 cm (1½ in) up the centre line from the yoke stitching line on both front and back pattern pieces (diagram 1).

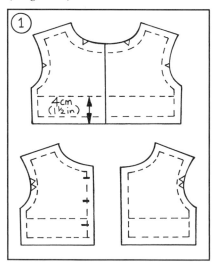

Trace the oval motif from page 49 onto the plain paper, ensuring that the centre front lines correspond exactly. Trace the corner motifs onto the corners of the front and back patterns (diagram 2).

Depending on the amount of space left between the centre front motif and the corner motifs, arrange the oval motif and the sprays of flowers to fill the space. Trace the motifs onto the paper pattern (diagram 3).

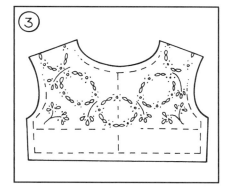

Repeat the arrangement for the back yoke, leaving sufficient room for buttons and buttonholes.

When the motifs are all in place, select initials and numbers for the child and the date of the celebration. Choose shapes which will work in satin stitch as for example the alphabet on page 65.

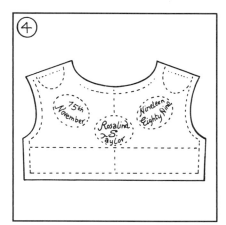

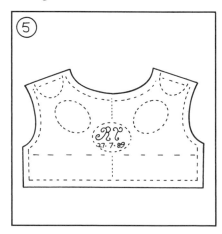

Take time to consider the placing of these letters and numerals as they are also design motifs. The initials and date might fit into the central oval motif but a long name with all the initials and a date in late November might result in a rather crowded motif. In this case, consider placing the initials in the central motif and the day and month in the left-hand motif with the year in the right-hand motif. Suggested arrangements are shown in diagrams 4 and 5.

METHOD

When the choice of initials and motifs has been made, trace them onto the pattern. Draw over all the lines with a smudge-proof black pen to ensure that the entire design can be seen through the fabric when the design is transferred. The design is now ready for transfer onto the fabric.

Using the commercial pattern, mark the yoke shapes onto the chosen fabric. Water-soluble pen or tacking can be used for the marking. Do not cut out at this stage.

When the garment shapes are marked on the fabric, place over the design so that the garment shapes correspond exactly. Pin carefully with brass pins. Transfer the design onto the yoke with dry, tinted poster paint and a small brush, or a water-soluble pen (page 86). Take great care as broderie anglaise relies on so many tiny shapes and it is important not to miss any.

Place the fabric in a tambour frame (page 86), tighten carefully and work the design as described in the skill file (page 44). Use two strands of cotton. Start with the tiny eyelets made with the stiletto, then the larger cut shapes and, finally, the French knots and padded satin stitch.

When all the embroidery is completed, press carefully and remove any traces of poster paint or water-soluble pen with a clean damp cloth or a cotton bud.

The yoke can now be cut out and the garment made up according to the commercial pattern instructions. The embroidery motifs could also be worked elsewhere on the garment – around the hem, on the cuffs, as a panel down the front or on a bonnet. The oval motifs are principally to enclose the initials and dates of babies and their christenings but could, of course, enclose other motifs of the embroiderer's choice.

Take care when making up the gown to use stitches and sewing thread that will not irritate a delicate skin. The white christening gown can look exceptionally attractive if worn over a simple gown, made like a detachable lining, of a soft pastel colour. The cut areas of the broderie anglaise are then displayed to their best advantage with little dashes of colour among the delicate stitchery. In this case the white gown will need to be slightly larger to fit.

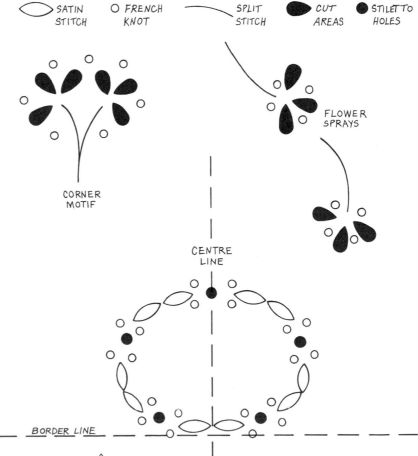

WINDOW DECAL

Broderie anglaise is a technique which is automatically associated with practical items. However, the current emphasis on decorating windows with richly draped curtains, lace half-curtains, tie-backs, Austrian and festoon blinds, has turned the craftworker's attention to the window as a display area.

Stained and painted glass, cut paper, punched metal and wrought iron have all been used to make decorative decals to hang in windows. The delicacy and cut areas of broderie anglaise make it an ideal technique for such decals. With daylight behind, the cut areas give a doyley-like appearance; at night, the work takes on a totally different look and the rich stitchery dominates.

The choice of design source for a decal is endless; from a replica of a motif in the curtains hung at the same window to a favourite view from a holiday. The choice of shape in which to enclose the work is also wide but the simplest, both in availability and making-up, is a circle. The choice of shape also governs the design of the work and a circular frame best complements a circular design.

REQUIREMENTS

Purchased metal ring, or commercial frame
Sufficient white cotton lawn to fit the frame
1 skein of white stranded cotton or silk
Purchased bias binding or sufficient fabric to make a bias strip wide enough to cover the frame
Size 10 sharps needle
A 23 cm (9 in) tambour frame
White and coloured poster paint and a fine brush
Stiletto

Place the fabric over the design on page 54 and transfer with dry, tinted poster paint or water-soluble transfer pen. Take care to transfer accurately as each mark forms part of the delicate design. Place the fabric in a tambour frame and tighten (page 86).

Look at the skill file for more detailed instructions (page 44). Pierce the eyelets with the stiletto, taking care not to make too large a hole. Using two strands of cotton, stitch all the eyelets including the flower centres and the seed heads.

Sew a running stitch around all the areas to be cut.

Carefully cut the small petals with a little slash and overcast the edges.

Work the padding, then the satin stitching for all the solid areas.

Work all the French knots around the flowers and the seed heads.

Work all the stem stitching for the stalks and seed heads.

Remove the fabric from the tambour frame and press carefully on the wrong side through a clean damp cloth. Remove any traces of transfer pen with a clean damp cloth or a cotton bud.

Place the embroidered fabric in the frame in which it will hang in the window. If it is a commercial frame, follow the instructions. If a plain metal or plastic circle is to be used, place the fabric right side down on a clean surface. Place the circle onto the fabric, making sure that the

space between the embroidery and the frame is equal all round.

Carefully fold the fabric over the frame at the 'north', 'south', 'east' and 'west' positions and, using brass pins, pin carefully (diagram 1).

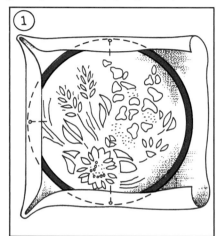

Repeat the folding until all the fabric is turned over and pinned (diagram 2).

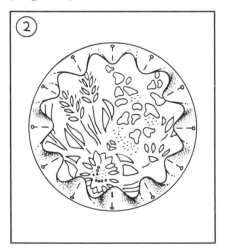

Adjust the pinning to ensure a tight fit without distorting the frame.

Tack just inside the frame, catching the folds down evenly, then use a fine stab stitch to secure the fabric (diagram 3).

Clip the fabric away to leave 1 cm (½ in) all round.

To encase the raw edges, a bias-cut strip is the most accommodating for a curved frame. A bias strip cut from the same fabric as the embroidery will give a neat, tailored look. A commercial, white satin bias binding would give a subtle contrast in surface appearance or a strip could be cut from a coloured fabric to co-ordinate with the room. Pin the chosen bias around the framed embroidery on the right side, with the raw edges away from the frame (diagram 4). Make a small fold across the beginning of the strip; the end of the strip is lain over this fold and is enclosed when the bias strip is folded over the frame.

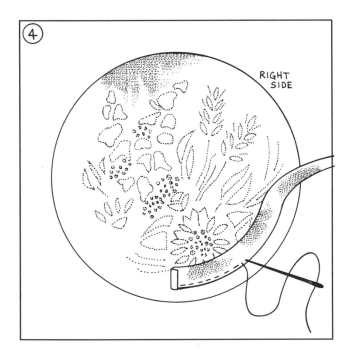

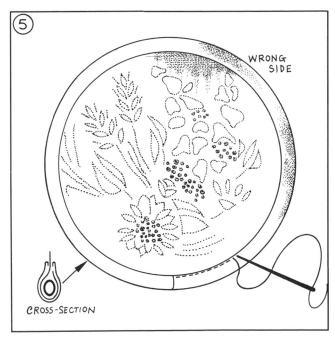

Neatly stab stitch the bias strip to the embroidered fabric, keeping the stitches exactly on the folded edge of the strip and against the inner edge of the frame.

Fold the bias strip over the frame and pin the second folded edge to the wrong side, enclosing the raw edges of the bias strip and the embroidered fabric. Ensure that the fold line lies exactly along the row of stitches (diagram 5). Neatly stab stitch the bias strip into place with a matching thread.

The decal is now completed. If you are not using a commercial frame with hanger, a simple commercial cord could be stitched to the bias binding (diagram 6). Tiny tassels could decorate each side but care

must be taken to see that any extra decoration does not overwhelm the main embroidery. The delicacy of the embroidered decal could be complemented by a fine cord and tassels made from the threads used for the embroidery, as shown in the skill file (pages 88 and 89).

The idea of the window decal design could be extended to the edges of a small 'cafe' curtain or a screen for a tiny window to obscure an unattractive view. Use the decal idea for a repeating motif or enlarge the design to fill the space.

The decal itself could contain a more detailed study of one flower or a spray of flowers. Use cut areas for the largest shapes, particularly petals, the characteristic eyelets for buds or the centre of a flower, satin stitch for the more complex shapes and stem stitch and French knots to complete the effect.

PADDED SATIN
STITCH

OVERSEWN CUT SHAPE

OVERSEWN STILETTO HOLE

FRENCH KNOT

STEM STITCH

E X P E R I M E N T I N G

Sources for ideas are endless but the character of the technique does lead to naturalistic designs. Flowers are the obvious choice and provide a range from the tiny sprig to the regal herbaceous border. Look at other sources of rich decoration: iron work; Roccoco architecture and carpet designs could all lead to exciting patterns for pieces of embroidery.

Broderie anglaise does not really translate well out of its original scale but can be worked on a fine wool. It works well on other colours but matching thread is essential.

An early twentieth century baby's gown machine-embroidered on cotton lawn showing a marvellous range of patterns

Several of the traditional whitework techniques are visually very similar to lace. Embroidery on net is sometimes confused with lace and, at its most intricate, is almost indistinguishable from it. Lace, however, constructs the whole fabric whereas net embroidery embellishes selected areas of manufactured net.

Net embroidery has a history which stretches back to the thirteenth century with references to darned nets for ecclesiastical use. Nowadays, the distinction is made between net embroidery, which is worked by machine, and net darning, which is the handsewn version. The technique has survived by changing to suit the fabric construction. Originally worked on square mesh (buratto) net and known as lacis or filet work, its popularity continued in various forms to the eighteenth century. The introduction of fine fabrics from India and the Far East at first usurped net embroidery but the fine embroidery techniques, also from the East, became popular and tambour, or chain stitch, appeared on net. In 1809, a machine was invented in Leicestershire in England which could produce net, and once again net became the vehicle for embroidery.

Throughout the history of embroidery, net has reflected change and, in the last quarter of the twentieth century, there is a dual approach to net. Scientific advances have produced various water soluble fabrics and exciting threads, *and* there is intense interest in embroidery and its history. Included under the same description of net embroidery are vibrant experimental handmade nets reflecting contemporary developments in crafts, and exquisitely filigree darned nets echoing the rich history of the technique.

Fabrics and threads

Net embroidery requires little equipment except the net, a needle and thread (for hand or machine sewing). It also requires a patient determination.

A wide variety of hexagonal nets are available and, for these projects, quality is the only requirement. Net can vary from very economical nylon net used for stiffening skirts, through a softer nylon, to cotton tulle and the finest quality silk for bridal veiling. In all cases the quality should be checked by pushing a stiletto through one of the hexagonal holes; the hole should stretch but no thread should be broken. Square net is occasionally available and is embroidered with stitches in a manner similar to pattern darning.

The choice of hand embroidery threads is almost unrestricted as the stitching is purely decorative and has no constructional purpose. Traditionally, a fine cotton or linen thread was used but, with the variety available today, the choice is at the discretion of the worker. For a distinctive design or pattern, use coton à broder, soft embroidery thread or perlé. For a fine filigree effect, a single, or a couple, of strands of stranded cotton work well. For textural effect, Natesh, Madeira or any of the glossy threads, angora or mohair knitting yarn and fine Russia braids or tiny ribbons can be very effective. The only restriction may be the weight that these threads add if the embroidered article is to drape.

For machine embroidery, restrict the thread to machine embroidery cotton, 30s or 50s only, or the fine iridescent and metallic thread made for the purpose. Do not attempt to use other threads designed for machine embroidery as thicker threads will tear the net to shreds.

Method for hand embroidery

It is not possible to transfer designs onto net but its transparent nature means that any design can be seen through the fabric.

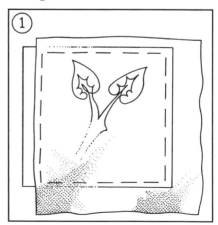

The chosen design is drawn clearly on white paper with a blue line (less trying to the eyes than black) and the net is placed over the design and tacked in place (diagram 1).

Using a tapestry needle, the design is worked with small darning stitches; in and out of the hexagonal hole nearest to the design line (diagram 2).

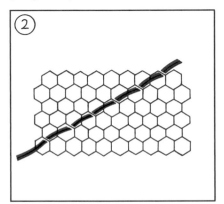

At no time is a knot used; the thread is woven in alongside an existing row of stitching. The first stitches are darned in along the design and overlapped when the motif is worked. The tension of the stitching is important and should be just tight enough to keep the design clear and unpuckered. Finish the thread by weaving into stitches at the back of the work.

The darning technique is used throughout the work following the lines of the design and counting the threads of net where a repeat pattern is used. Because the net is hexagonal, care is needed when working a design vertically instead of the customary horizontal manner. The shape may alter.

Method for machine embroidery

The design is drawn on tissue paper, placed under the net and the machine embroidery is worked through the net *and* the tissue paper. The tissue is torn away when the embroidery is complete.

Because machine embroidery must be worked in a tambour frame, each design motif must be not larger than 20 cm (8 in); the largest frame advisable for the work is 23 cm (9 in). Overlapping a design is not advisable as it is extremely difficult to achieve accuracy.

Place the net carefully into the bottom of a tambour frame (page 86) ensuring that the frame encloses the area where the motif is to be positioned. Never pull the net too hard when tightening the frame as the net may easily tear. Gently ease the fabric until it is taut.

Draw the motif on tissue paper ensuring that the motif will fit inside the tambour frame.

Pin, then tack the tissue under the net in the tambour frame, checking the position of the motif (diagram 3). Remove the pins.

Place the frame under the needle of the machine and bring the bobbin thread through to the surface of the net by holding the top thread taut whilst moving the wheel by hand (diagram 4).

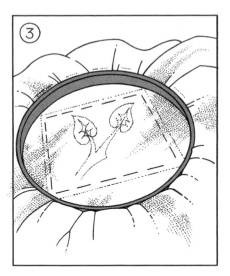

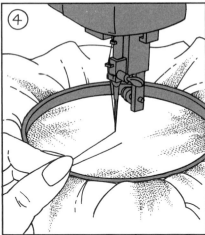

Stitch the motif by outlining first, then return to fill in extra details, e.g. veins on leaves. When the motif is complete, leave long threads and remove the frame from the machine. Repeat the procedure for all the motifs.

Carefully remove the tissue paper using tweezers if necessary. Hand knot all loose ends.

Yoke

The insertion of a handsewn embroidered yoke into a white dress is a way of introducing embroidery to a dress that might otherwise be undecorated. Net embroidery is ideal for a wedding dress made in a richly textured silk or heavily figured damask where too much embroidery would be overwhelming, or for a confirmation dress where heavy embroidery would be unsuitable.

REQUIREMENTS

Commercial pattern, see below
Sufficient dress net to make yoke (check with commercial pattern first)

Fabric to complete the pattern
A selection of threads to darn the net, e.g. coton à broder, perlé cotton,

stranded cotton
White sewing thread
Size 22 tapestry needle
A sheet of plain paper
Pencils, blue felt-tip pen

WORKING THE EMBROIDERY

Select a commercial dress pattern with a square yoke and back opening. Trace the front and back yoke pattern onto a sheet of plain paper. Mark the centre front of the yoke and all seam allowances and notches, dots, etc.

Trace the centre motif onto the front of the yoke then continue to trace the corner motifs on front and back (page 61).

Avoiding the shoulder seams, make an arrangement of the sprig and bow motifs in the spaces left (diagram 1). This will obviously vary depending on the size of the yoke.

Draw over the transferred motifs with a fine blue line.

Using the commercial pattern, cut out the yoke sections in net, leaving generous seam allowances.

Mark the seam lines with tacking stitches in a contrasting coloured sewing thread.

Pin, then tack the corresponding yoke pieces onto the paper, matching the seam lines (diagram 2).

Using a firm thread, e.g. coton à broder, darn the outlines of the design, starting each thread as described in the skill file (page 57).

When the outline darning is completed, darn the fine details with a finer thread, e.g. one strand of stranded cotton or a glossy thread.

When all the work on the yoke sections is completed, press carefully on the wrong side.

MAKING UP

Make up the yoke section as described in the commercial pattern instructions. As net can be quite brittle, it might be advisable to bind

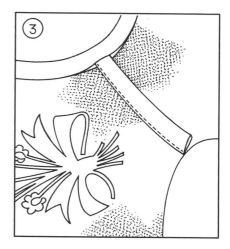

all the seams to prevent the net from irritating the skin of the wearer (diagram 3).

The three motifs used for the yoke can easily be adapted for other garments. A scattering of bows and flowers on dark, stiff net for the overskirt of a brilliantly coloured evening dress could then be further embellished with beads and sequins. Similarly, a veil for a hat would look delicious with the bows discreetly placed along the edge.

CENTRE
MOTIF

CORNER MOTIF

BRIDAL VEIL

Veils are the finishing touch to the entire wedding outfit
and vary tremendously; from tiny wisps that just
cover the face of the bride to yards of tulle requiring
attendants to carry it in procession.

All styles offer the opportunity for delicate embroidery. It is important to consider the position of the veil, both before and after the actual ceremony, and equally, the position of any embroidery. An embroidered motif on the front of the veil must not obscure the bride's vision and must complement the head-dress and hair-style when the veil is thrown back. Similarly, scattered motifs around the hem of a medium-length veil must be considered in conjunction with the back of the dress. Details such as a plunging back or a large bow at the waist, are all important to the balance of the design.

The real pleasure in creating a hand-made item is two-fold; the actual process of embroidery and the unique nature of the article being produced. When embroidery is being worked for a celebration, a third element is added because the work is for a specific person. In the case of a wedding, a particular couple are commemorated and the design can include details especially for them. In this basic design, to which other details could be added, a dozen rose motifs are scattered around the hem to form a border. A heart-shaped motif is placed in the centre to take the initials of the couple and the date of the wedding.

REQUIRERMENTS

Sufficient silk net (tulle) for a veil of the chosen length and width	2 reels of 30s or 50s white machine embroidery cotton thread Size 80 machine needle	A 23 cm (9 in) tambour frame Tissue paper Water-soluble blue pen

---

Using a contrasting coloured sewing thread, mark the centre line of the veil and also a line 23 cm (9 in) in and parallel to the edge of the veil for the border. The centre line needs to be marked with tacking to show the distance from the edge to the position chosen for the heart motif.

The border needs to be marked so that the 'start' and 'finish' are parallel to the centre line, i.e. at the point where the curves straighten out, forming a semi-circle in which to position the motifs (diagram 1).

removed. Do not use felt-tip pen or pencil. Trace the couple's initials and the date of the wedding, using an alphabet such as the one shown to fit within the heart. A continuous script is easier: separate letters will require a start and finish for each letter.

Place the heart motif under the net in the desired position, with the centre line of tacking corresponding to the centre line of the heart motif. Tack the tissue to the net and place in a tambour frame (page 86).

Trace twelve rose motifs (page 66) and place in an informal pattern over the tacked border line, with six either side of the heart motif. Tack stitch to the net (diagram 2).

Machine embroider in the same way as the heart motif.

Add any personal touches but take care not to clutter the design. All designs for machine embroidery on net should be simple and flowing. Formal geometric shapes are not successful.

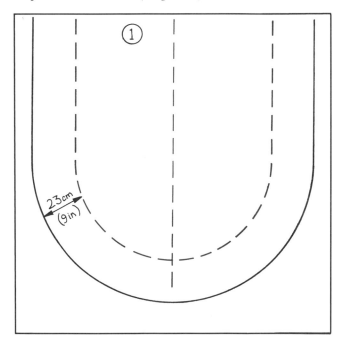

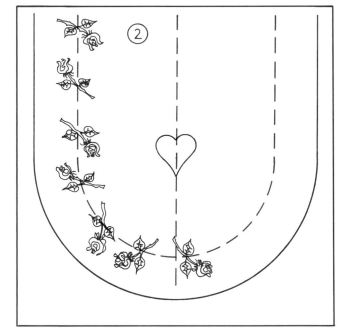

Trace the heart motif from page 65, onto tissue paper with a water-soluble pen. This ensures that if any of the drawing medium is inadvertently transferred onto the machine thread, it can easily be

Following the directions in the skill file for machine embroidery (page 57), machine embroider the heart shape, numerals and letters, beginning at the base of the heart and stitching the inner line first.

The roses could, of course, be replaced by any favourite flower or group of flowers as long as the shape is kept simple and the embroidery motif is produced as a continuous outline.

CENTRE LINE

abcdefghijklmnopqrstuvwxyz

1234567890

EXPERIMENTING

Although embroidery on net is a little limited by the structure of the fabric, ideas can still be realized in some exciting ways. The stitchery and threads are entirely decorative and a wide range of fibres could be darned into the net. The only restrictions would be the eventual use for the embroidered net and the weight of the darned fibres. The embroidery could also be further enriched with tiny beads to support the darning. Very large beads and sequins should be avoided when working on a delicate technique. Net darning can work well in all the colours available but always use a matching thread.

Machine-embroidered net is similar to darned net except the bulkier fibres could not be used in the machine. The wealth of shaded, metallic and iridescent machine threads could look magnificent suspended on net but always use matching or toning threads. A contrasting thread will look terribly spotty.

A worked sample of the effect achieved by darning on net with a thicker range of fibres

SHADOW WORK AND SHADOW APPLIQUE

The light, elegant effect of shadow work is created by the use of applied transparent fabrics and delicate stitchery worked from the wrong side. The Indian influence on the original traditional work so popular in the mid-nineteenth century, gives a rich inheritance of pattern and technique. Designs from floral and architectural sources are excellent for shadow work, offering a variety of shapes and depth to display the use of fabric and stitchery to the full.

Fabrics and threads

Organdie (cotton), organza (silk), muslin, crêpe de Chine, fine linen, lawn, voile, georgette, and fine synthetic, transparent fabrics of a reasonably firm construction are all ideal. Avoid knitted fabrics and transparent fabrics which have a 'floppy' character as they may prove rather difficult to work. Equally, a very stiff fabric will prove unwieldy and will detract from the flowing lines of the stitchery.

The range of threads now available allow the embroiderer a wonderful choice for shadow work.

Traditionally, the equivalent of one strand of stranded cotton, coton à broder, or perlé was used but a fine crewel wool, pure silk, a fine floss, or a matt flower thread could all also be used to enhance this delicate technique.

Method

Every embroidery technique inherits such a wealth of fabrics, designs and uses that, while avoiding repetition for tradition's sake, an awareness of this inheritance can guide the embroiderer towards successful choices. Thus, the tradition of shadow work in monochromatic colours (predominantly white), fine threads, flowing elegant designs and for practical use are all excellent indicators for contemporary designs and articles.

Designs should have narrow shapes and flowing lines to allow the stitches, usually herringbone, to realize their full potential. An

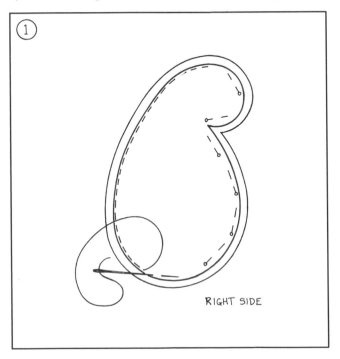

RIGHT SIDE

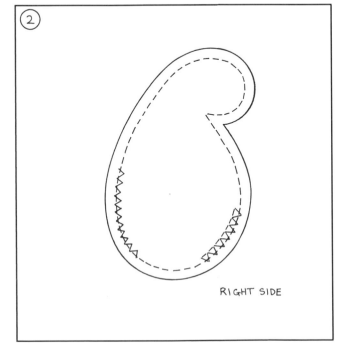

RIGHT SIDE

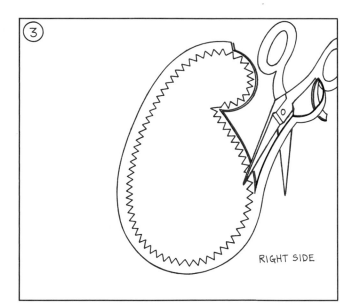

RIGHT SIDE

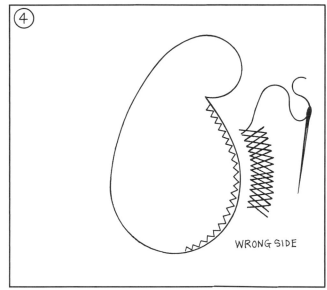

WRONG SIDE

overcomplicated line detracts from the intricacy of the technique and wide shapes produce overlong and ugly stitches.

Although shadow work has an almost ethereal quality, its delicacy masks its strength. Because the stitches are small and there are no areas of weakened fabric, it is an immensely practical technique and launders well. Traditionally, shadow work has been used for clothing, including infants' and children's, and household linen.

All shadow work should follow this sequence which helps to avoid potential problems.

Transfer the design onto the main fabric and also onto any fabric to be appliquéd, ensuring the grain is parallel on all pieces. Transfer can be with dry, white poster paint and

brush, or with a water-soluble pen (page 86).

Cut out all the pieces of fabric to be appliquéd, leaving a 3 mm (⅛ in) allowance round the edge to be trimmed when the stitching is completed.

Carefully pin the appliquéd pieces to the main fabric using brass pins and checking that the grains of the fabrics are parallel. Tack together with small tacking stitches, just inside the design lines (diagram 1).

Attach the appliquéd fabric to the right side with a decorative machine stitch and a spear point needle, or with hand embroidery using pin stitch or herringbone stitch (page 90). Use a betweens or crewel needle depending on the thread and fabric (diagram 2).

Using very sharp embroidery scissors, clip away any surplus fabric (diagram 3).

Work herringbone stitch on the wrong side for additional decoration and for linear detail. Herringbone is the ideal stitch, adapting to curves and allowing a design to flow without restriction (diagram 4). Very fine linear detail can be added with the use of back stitch.

Remove any visible poster-paint or pen marks using a clean, damp cloth or cotton bud.

BOOK COVER

Although shadow work looks delicate, it is hardwearing
and well-suited to articles that may need laundering.
Book bindings are both precious and expensive to repair,
and a cover is an ideal way of preserving the binding. This
cover is intended for a small book, such as a prayer book,
but it could be used for any book for a special occasion.

The Indian origins of shadow work provide a
beautiful source of designs. The rich, flowing
lines of Indian architecture are well suited to
the dimensions of a book cover and the
technique captures the cool, airy atmosphere
of some of the Indian palaces. The design of
the book cover has been created to be adapted
to fit any size of book from a minimum of
10 cm × 10 cm (4 in × 4 in), to a maximum of
15 cm × 20 cm (6 in × 8 in).

REQUIREMENTS

25 cm (10 in) white silk
  organza
1 skein of white stranded
  cotton or silk
Size 10 betweens needle

A 23 cm (9 in) tambour
  frame
Tracing paper
White and coloured poster
  paint and a fine brush

MEASURING UP

Measure the size of the book to be covered and draw a pattern to the following dimensions onto tracing paper:

Height The height of the book plus 2.5 cm (1 in) turnings top and bottom.

Width 8 cm (3 in) plus the width of the book, plus 6 mm (¼ in), plus the width of the spine, plus 6 mm (¼ in), plus the width of the book, plus 8 cm (3 in).

This allows for turnings top and bottom, a flap for the front and back cover, and an allowance for ease at the spine (diagram 1).

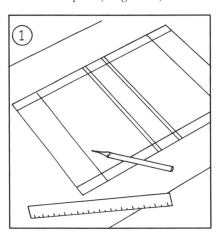

MAKING UP

Trace the motif from page 73 into the four corners of the front and back covers and draw with a firm black line.

Placing the pattern underneath, pin, then tack the straight lines on the

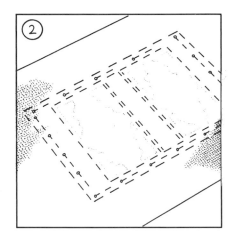

organza (diagram 2). It is important to try to keep the straight edges of the pattern along the straight grain of the fabric.

Next transfer the corner designs with tinted, dry poster paint and a fine brush, or a water-soluble pen (page 86), onto both front and back cover areas. Remove the pins.

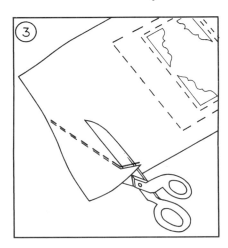

From a small piece of organza cut out eight corners to be appliquéd onto the main cover (diagram 3).

Transfer the corner design onto this fabric eight times and cut these out carefully a little outside the transferred line (diagram 4).

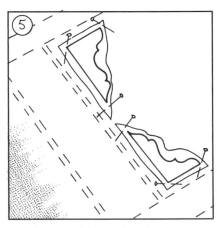

With brass pins, place these pieces of fabric in the appropriate places on the right side of the main cover (diagram 5). Using a small stitch,

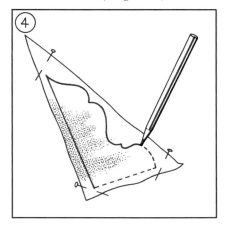

tack into position. Place in the frame.

Using pin stitch (page 90) and one strand of cotton, attach the fabric pieces to the main cover along the curving and straight edges (diagram 6). Clip away the surplus fabric using sharp embroidery scissors.

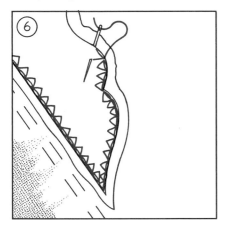

Using herringbone stitch, embroider along the straight edge and around the design, following the second line (diagram 7).

Remove all traces of the design transfer and press on the wrong side

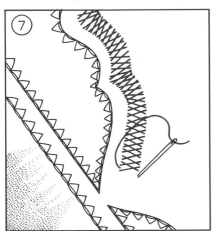

with a clean, damp cloth. Carefully cut out the book cover along the outer tack lines.

Press the hem allowance to the right side around the whole piece, mitring the corners (see page 87), and tack down.

Using pin stitch, stitch along the entire hem 3 mm (⅛ in) from the edges. Trim excess fabric.

Fold the front and back cover flaps in, wrong side together, and loosely oversew the edges (diagram 8).

With a very fine needle and thread, oversew the edges together with tiny stitches. Remove the loose oversewing.

The cover is now complete and ready for use. Open the book to be

used and lay first one cover and then the second into the flaps and then close the book. The 6 mm (¼ in) ease allows the book to close.

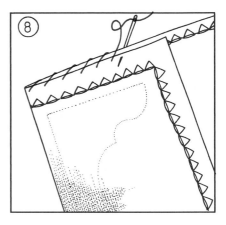

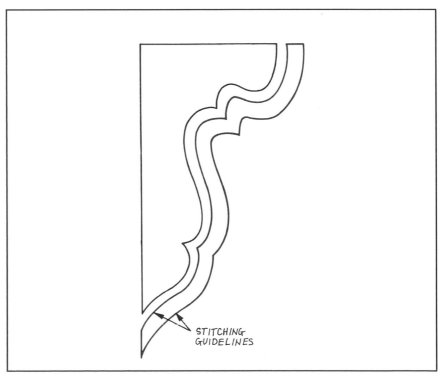

STITCHING GUIDELINES

CHILD'S PINAFORE

A special outfit can be created for a child by placing an
embroidered pinafore over a fairly plain dress. The pinafore
may well last for years while the sleeve and dress lengths
become too short.

A dainty pinafore in organdie will also be ideal
for different seasons and, will look equally
charming over a printed cotton lawn with
short sleeves, or a dark-coloured velvet or
wool with long sleeves. Despite its delicate
appearance, shadow work will launder well,
aided by the use of cotton organdie rather than
silk organza. It is advisable to wash the
organdie before the embroidery is started as
cotton fabrics can shrink.

REQUIREMENTS

Commercial pattern (see
  below)
Sufficient white cotton
  organdie to make the
  pinafore (check with the
commercial pattern first)
1 skein of white stranded
  cotton
White sewing thread
Size 10 betweens needle
A 23 cm (9 in) tambour
  frame
A large sheet of plain paper
White and coloured poster
  paint and a fine brush

Select a commercial pattern for a child's pinafore with a high waistline and a back opening to fit the child but be generous in the choice of size. The work may take a while to complete and children grow very fast.

Trace the commercial skirt pattern onto a sheet of plain paper, marking all the notches, etc.

Draw a line 10 cm (4 in) up from the hem line.

Mark the centre front and centre back lines (diagram 1).

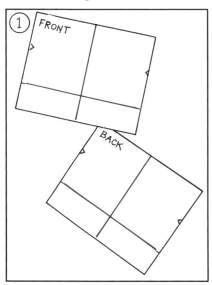

Trace the design from page 77 onto the paper pattern, ensuring that the centre line of the design lies on the centre front and centre back line of the garment pattern.

Repeat the design along the border line fitting in enough repeats to fill the area (diagram 2).

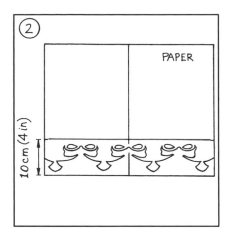

Using the commercial pattern, cut out the skirt, allowing a 10 cm (4 in) hem (diagram 3). Mark notches and hem lines with tailor tacks.

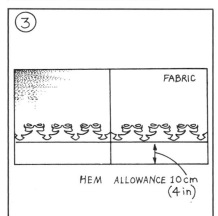

Stitch the side seams using a French seam (page 87). If there is no back seam, only stitch one side seam leaving the skirt as one flat piece of fabric.

Pin the skirt to the design with brass pins, matching centre front, centre back and hem lines.

Transfer the design with tinted, dry poster paint, or water-soluble pen.

Carefully press along the fold for the hem to the right side and tack in position.

Place in the frame. Using pin stitch (page 90) and one strand of cotton, follow the design along the entire hem. This stitches the hem and gives a decorative finish (diagram 4).

Trim away any surplus fabric, using very sharp embroidery scissors.

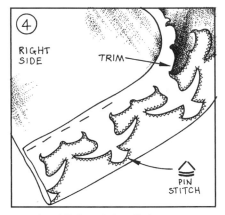

Work additional details in herringbone stitch on the wrong side and with the work in the frame (diagram 5).

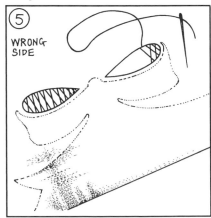

METHOD

Press work on the wrong side through a clean, damp cloth and remove any traces of transfer with a cloth or a cotton bud.

Stitch the remaining seam of the skirt pattern, using a French seam and catch stitch the seam to the hem.

The embroidery is now complete and the pinafore can be made up using the commercial pattern instructions.

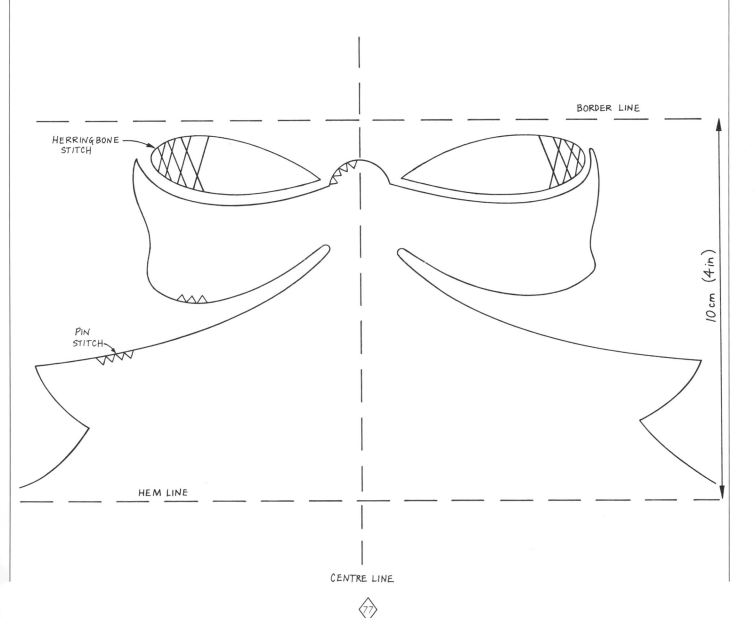

BORDER LINE

HERRINGBONE STITCH

PIN STITCH

HEM LINE

CENTRE LINE

10cm (4in)

The elegance of shadow work offers a wealth of possibilities for further ideas. Eastern architecture offers sumptuous curves and delicate pinnacles which look wonderful when worked in the sheer fabrics used for shadow work.

Silhouettes are another ideal source for designs and can often be found on the endpapers of children's books. Simplified, these could be delightful for a cushion cover or a lampshade. All the patterns could be worked in other colours and could even be further embellished without detracting from the shadow work.

The jacket could be made in a soft rich colour with a matching metallic machine thread used for the stitching. Avoid dark colours, apart from black, as the shadow effect tends to be lost. A spear point needle may cause

the metallic thread to fray so it is always wise to experiment first before committing oneself to working the actual piece of fabric.

The child's pinafore could be very pretty if soft colours were used or, perhaps a soft colour for the appliqué on a white organdie. Try delicate coloured thread for the herringbone stitch. The motif, if slightly adapted as shown below, could also be used on its own on a pocket, for example.

The book cover could be adapted to suit a special anniversary by stitching the herringbone in silver or gold. A symbol could be introduced into the middle of the design, e.g. a monogram, a crucifix, a special flower, a Star of David or a particular date to make the cover a personal gift.

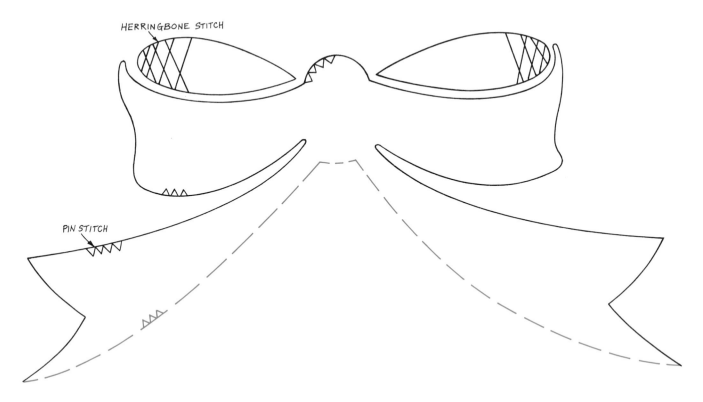

HERRINGBONE STITCH

PIN STITCH

Extending the technique: this spray of flowers commemorates a wedding and was inspired by the bride's bouquet using fabrics and beads from her dress (kindly loaned by Margeth Lingwood)

JACKET

Weddings have always been a marvellous opportunity for
display and many brides choose an outfit that can be worn on
other occasions. The addition of a delicate transparent
jacket over a sleeveless or strapless dress would create
an original and stunning combination.

Because the jacket will be transparent and
elegantly decorated, the dress should be simple
in design and complementary in the use of
fabric. An organza jacket with a wild silk
dress, lawn over crisp linen, georgette floating
over silk ottoman; all give a combination
where the fabrics complement one another and
support the intricacy of the embroidery.

REQUIREMENTS

Commercial jacket pattern, see
  below
Sufficient silk organza to make
  the jacket (check with
  commercial pattern first) plus
  50 cm (½ yard) for borders
1 skein of white stranded cotton

or stranded silk
Matching sewing thread
4 reels of white machine
  embroidery thread
Spear point machine
  embroidery needles
Size 10 betweens needle

A 18 cm (7 in) tambour frame
Several sheets of plain paper
  and a fine brush
White and coloured poster paint
Tracing paper
Thin card or equivalent

WORKING THE EMBROIDERY

Select a commercial pattern for a loose, untailored cardigan with a V-neck. Trace the pattern pieces for the front, back, side panels (if included) and sleeve sections onto a large piece of plain paper.

Draw a line to form a border on this new pattern all around the edge of the jacket measuring in from the stitching line 5 cm (2 in) deep for a size 10 to 8 cm (3 in) deep for a size

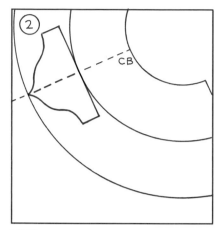

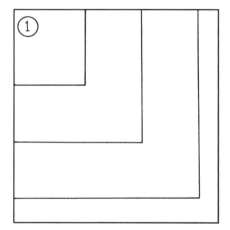

24. Draw another line 6 cm (2½ in) inside the first line (diagram 1).

Trace the pattern for the border of the jacket onto tracing paper.

Trace the border motif and the Paisley motif from page 85. Use the tracing as a template and cut out several of each in stiff paper or thin card.

Place the border motif in the following positions on the copied garment pattern, with the base line

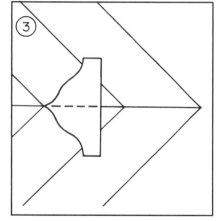

of the template resting on the first border line and the point touching the second border line:

(1) Centre back neckline and hemline (diagram 2).

(2) Diagonally in each corner (diagram 3). Draw round these motifs.

(3) Avoiding shoulder, side and sleeve seams, place motifs at equal distances between these first four points, then repeat this

arrangement around the sleeve hem. Draw round these motifs (diagram 4).

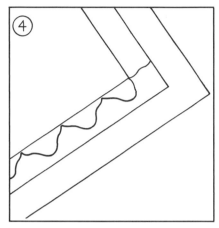

(4) Mark points on the second border line halfway between each border motif (diagram 5). Place the Paisley motif on these points with the line A–B at 90° to the border line. Draw round the motifs (diagram 6).

The design is now transferred onto the copy pattern.

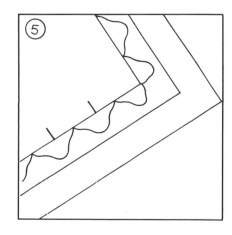

Using the commercial pattern, cut out the garment, marking all the notches, etc. with tailor tacks.

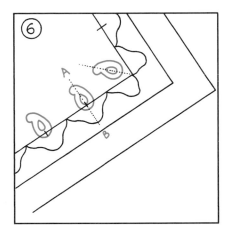

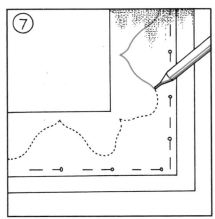

Using the tracing of the border, cut out the border pieces for the jacket and sleeves in the same fabric, adding a 3 mm (⅛ in) seam allowance.

Carefully place the garment pieces over the corresponding copied pattern and pin to the paper.

Transfer the border motif and

Paisley motif onto the main garment pieces (page 86).

Repeat the transfer procedure with the border design and the border pieces (diagram 7).

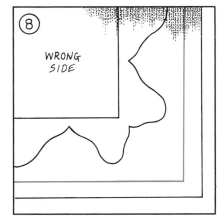

Using French seams, stitch the shoulder seams on the main garment pieces and the border pieces (page 87).

Press the seams towards the back of the jacket.

Stitch the border pieces to the main garment pieces (wrong sides together) around the neck, down the fronts, along the back hem and round the sleeve hems, with a 1.5 cm (⅝ in) seam allowance (diagram 8).

Clip the seam allowances to 1 cm (½ in) and turn the border pieces to the outside of the main garment pieces (diagram 9). Take great care to clip all the curves and corners. Try to avoid stretching the raw edges of the border pieces.

Carefully press the seams flat.

Matching the transferred lines on the main garment pieces and the border pieces, tack the two layers of fabric together using a small 1 cm to 2 cm (½ in to ¾ in) stitch just inside the edge of the design (diagram 10).

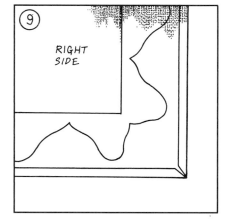

Using a spear point needle and a selected automatic stitch (or a medium zigzag stitch) with machine embroidery cotton both on top of the machine and in the bobbin, work a row of test stitching on a spare piece of fabric. Make any adjustments to tension, stitch size, etc. at this stage.

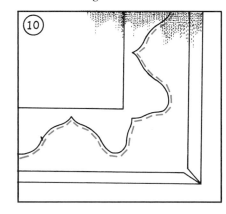

Taking great care, stitch along the transferred line to attach the edge of the border pieces to the main garment pieces (diagram 11). The decorative stitching and the regular holes created by the spear point needle create a rich edge to the border pattern. Ensure that all loose threads are well secured.

When all the machine stitching is completed, carefully clip around the edges of the border to remove any surplus fabric (diagram 12). Very sharp embroidery scissors must be used to ensure a successful result.

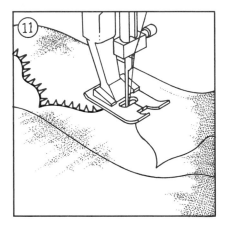

Carefully press the garment pieces on the wrong side, ironing through a clean damp cloth.

Using an 18 cm (7 in) tambour frame, place a section of the garment which has a Paisley motif in the frame and manoeuvre the fabric to achieve a suitable tautness. Great care must be taken, so that the fabric is not damaged.

Start with a few neat back stitches to secure the thread and work a fine herringbone stitch around the inside line of the motif. Work a vertical line of herringbone stitch to form the inside of the motif (diagram 13).

Finish each set of stitches by weaving the thread through the back of previous stitches.

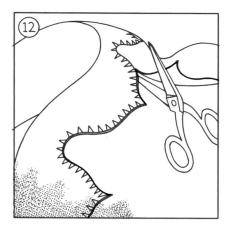

Complete all the Paisley motifs in the same way. Press in the same way as the border from the right side.

MAKING UP

When all the embroidery is complete, make up the jacket using French seams to enclose all the raw edges. If the jacket has set in sleeves, bind the seams with a bias strip, cut from remnants of the fabric. Press carefully with all the seams towards the back of the garment.

With a fine needle and thread, and small stitches, catch the seams to the borders at the side seams and sleeve edges (diagram 14).

Using the same machine stitch as used for the appliqué, carefully sew around the edge, 1 cm (½ in) in, along the clipped seam allowance (diagram 15). This adds a final detail

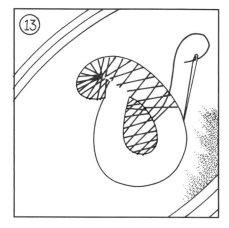

to the garment and gives a little firmness to the edges.

Using a clean damp cloth, cotton bud or swab, remove any remaining poster paint or water-soluble pen marks. Finally press all over, check the seams and all the embroidery for any unfinished threads.

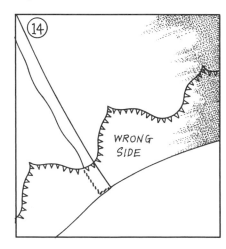

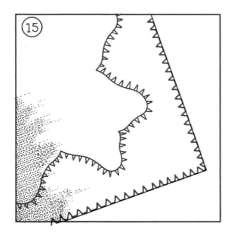

The embroidered garment is now ready. Left plain, it could be worn for day wear or, with the addition of tiny pearls or matt, white beads, scattered around the paisley motifs or along the border edges, it would translate well for evening wear.

The border idea is ideal for any items using sheer fabrics. A delicate bolero in chiffon in a colour to complement a patterned dress would add a unique touch: the paisley motif could be stitched in a darker shade of thread. At the other extreme a full-skirted long coat would also look marvellous with the border appliqué all round the edges.

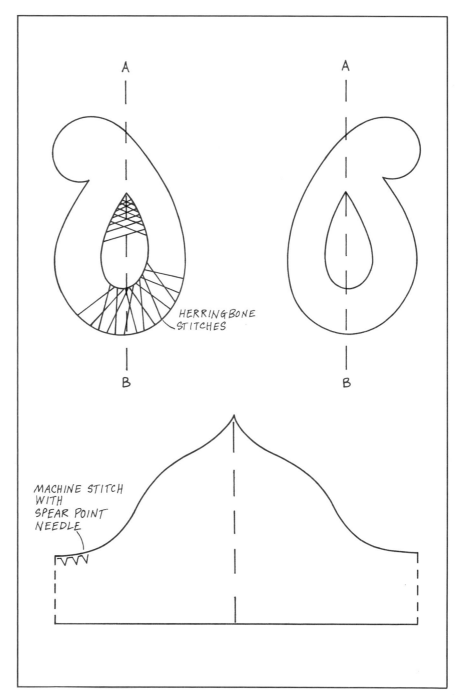

Transferring designs

Water soluble pens

Ensure that the pen purchased will work on the fabric to be used and that it is a non-smudge variety. The variety with ink that fades with time may not be safe on some fabrics.

Trace the design carefully onto paper with a fine black, smudge-proof pen. Allow the ink to dry thoroughly.

Place the fabric to be embroidered over the tracing and pin in place with the pins facing outwards. Carefully trace the design onto the fabric with a pen containing water-soluble ink. Blue ink is an easy colour to work with.

When the embroidery is completed, the tracing lines can be removed by laundering. If this is impractical, a fine mist of water from a sprayer will remove most of the tracing and the remainder can be removed with a dampened cotton bud.

Dry poster paint

A traditional method of transferring designs, which is particularly suitable for whitework. White poster paint and a fine brush are the essential equipment and access to a watercolour box or a small tablet of a dark colour to add tint if needed.

Pin the fabric in place over the traced design as above, then carefully trace the design onto the fabric, using the paint almost dry, only dampening the brush if

needed. If the pure white is not visible enough, take a good brushful of white paint onto a palette or similar and add a tiny dash of dark colour, just to tint the white. The painted line is far less distracting to the work in progress than a contrast transfer line. The dry paint flakes off as the line is stitched.

When the embroidery is completed, any remaining paint can be removed by gently rubbing a clean finger along the line.

Using a tambour frame

It is advisable to bind the inner ring with a very light fabric cut in bias strips. This binding helps to keep the fabric clean and maintain the tautness. If a very delicate piece of fabric is used, it is advisable to place a piece of tissue over the fabric before the outer ring is placed in position. The tissue can be torn away from the area to be worked. This helps to keep the work clean and avoids ring marks.

The fabric to be embroidered is placed over the inner ring, the outer ring is then placed over the fabric and, when the screw is tightened, the fabric is kept taut. The fabric may need to be gently manoeuvred to achieve required tautness. The tension will eventually slacken and the fabric will need tightening at frequent intervals.

Embroidery is usually worked with the right side of the embroidery

uppermost in the frame, except in the case of machine embroidery where the fabric must lie on the machine bed.

Dressing a frame – Most embroidery fabrics can be placed straight into the frame. If a very delicate fabric is to be used, first place a backing fabric, e.g. lawn, calico, organdie, in the frame, then stitch the delicate fabric to the backing, ensuring that the grain lines of the fabric are parallel. The backing can be carefully cut away to reveal the delicate fabric (diagram 1). This procedure can also be used if the work is too small to be placed in the frame.

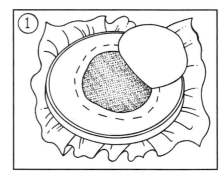

Pinning out or blocking

If the work has become distorted, the shape can be restored by patient pinning out. A piece of hardboard or plywood, slightly larger than the piece of work, blotting paper, brass (rust-proof) drawing pins, a water spray and a right angle or set square are required.

Pin the blotting paper to the board.

Dampen the embroidery, then pin one straight edge onto the board on top of the blotting paper, which will absorb the moisture.

Pin the centre of the opposite edge, then the centre of the two sides. Working outwards from the centre, pin the opposite edge, then the two sides, pulling gently into shape and using the right angle to check any 90° corners. Allow to dry.

If the distortion has not been totally removed, spray the work with a fine mist of water and repeat the blocking with the opposite edge and two sides. Allow to dry. Repeat until the shape is restored.

When the work is totally dry, remove and make up as required.

PRESSING

The iron is essential to the production of good embroidery and can also be its ruin. A high temperature or a dirty sole plate can cause disasters. Always check the temperature on a scrap of the fabric.

Always press from the wrong side. Pressing through a clean, damp cloth is a good safeguard. Make sure that the ironing board cover is clean or press onto a piece of clean fabric. Use the nose of the iron around stitching, taking care that the nose does not lift any of the stitches.

Press fine cotton on a glass or mirror for a slightly glazed finish.

A little spray starch can be added while pressing.

SEWING TECHNIQUES

Included here are several sewing techniques which will prove useful in the making up of articles.

French seams

A fine seam which is ideal for transparent fabrics. Working with the wrong sides together, sew a narrow seam and trim turnings carefully to a minimum. Turn the work to the wrong side and sew a second seam with right sides together, enclosing the raw edges (diagram 2).

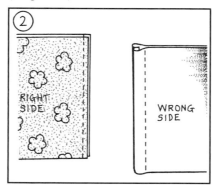

Tailor tacks

The original way of marking positions on garments through several layers of fabric at the same time. Work with a very long piece of sewing thread doubled and stitch along the line to be marked but leave each stitch as a loop on the surface. When the tacking is complete, gently move the layers of fabric apart and carefully clip the threads between the layers (diagram 3). The cut ends will now mark the positions.

Mitring corners

A sharp corner on the straight grain, with excess fabric cut away and the mitre neatly stitched, will complement a fine piece of embroidery. There are several different ways of achieving this but all have the same basis.

Establish the finished hem line and press. Establish the depth of hem and press. On large pieces of work, e.g. tablecloths, it is advisable to tack these lines if the hemming may take some time to complete.

Mark a line at 45° which cuts the corner, just above the inner folds.

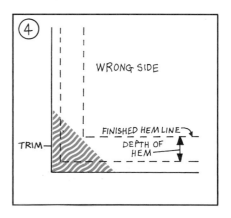

Trim excess fabric away, ensuring that a seam allowance is left inside the inner fold lines (diagram 4).

For even-weave fabrics, withdraw a thread from the fold line and the hem line. If a traditional hemstitched hem is required, withdraw the chosen number of threads from the main body of the embroidery along the line reached by the fold of the hem. Press the seam allowance, press along the outer hem line and then the inner hem line (diagram 5). Tack down and slip stitch across the mitred join.

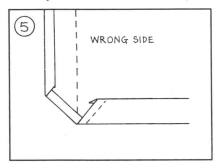

For closely-woven fabrics, work on the right side. Machine, stab stitch or back stitch the mitred join and turn through to the back of the work. Press and hem (diagram 6).

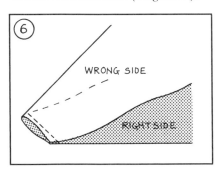

Decorative finishes

Cords

Any thread can be used for cord making, bearing in mind the use of the cord. Obviously, a cord for a shoulder bag must be made from a more hardwearing thread than a decorative addition to an elegant scatter cushion. A wide variety of threads can be twisted together to form cords but it is always advisable to make a test cord first. A thread which looks stunning in the hank can twist to nothing, and some threads are too stretchy and will never achieve sufficient twist to make a good cord.

Measure lengths of thread which are three times the required finished length, e.g. for a 120 cm (47 in) cord, cut threads 360 cm (141 in) long. A minimum of two lengths of thread are needed but any number can be used and the finished cord will have twice this number.

Knot the threads together at both ends. Ideally, another person is needed to wind but it is quite possible to make a cord with the assistance of a cup hook or door handle! Place one knotted end over a hook and place a pencil through the other end.

Hold the threads loosely between thumb and forefinger just behind the pencil. Pull the threads taut and start to twist the pencil round and round, as if winding up a balsa wood toy plane (diagram 7).

Always wind in a clockwise direction.

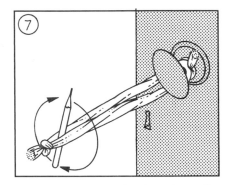

Continue twisting the threads until a kink appears. This indicates that sufficient tension has been achieved. Carefully take the pencil to the hook to fold the cord in half. Threading a weight onto the cord will help produce an even twist.

Hold the two knotted ends together with the pencil, so that the threads are vertical. The tension will now cause the two halves to spin together at great speed (diagram 8).

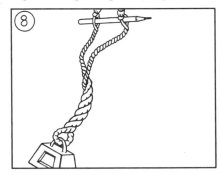

When the spinning has finished, remove from the hook and knot the cord just below the pencil and just above the loop at the other end. Cut the loop and trim both ends.

Tassels

Depending on the work which the tassel is to trim, the choice of size and thread is endless. For fine silk or plump wool, the technique is the same.

Cut a piece of firm card to the depth of the length of tassel required, and about twice as wide. Select the threads to be used and cut generous lengths. Holding the end of the card with thumb and forefinger, wind the threads firmly round the card sufficient times to achieve the thickness of tassel required. Extra thread can be added at any time, ensuring that the cut ends are always on the same side of the card. If there are to be several matching tassels, cut enough thread first and count the number of winds of each thread.

When the winding is finished, thread a blunt needle with matching thread and slide the needle under the threads at the top of the card (diagram 9).

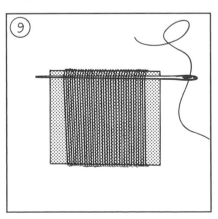

Pull this thread tight and knot it together. With sharp scissors, cut through all the threads on the opposite side, making sure that all the cut threads are held together at the top.

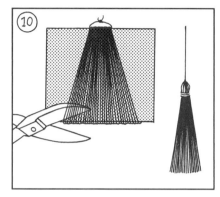

The tassel can now be simply finished off by taking the needle and thread tightly round the loose threads, then up through the middle to form a hanging thread (diagram 10).

Variations can be worked on the tassel if the embroidery calls for a richer decoration. A wooden bead can be inserted in the middle of the tassel to form a larger head. A buttonhole stitch can be worked spirally round the head, with a small bead on each stitch, for a highly decorated tassel.

Bias binding

A length of matching or co-ordinating fabric which is cut on the bias or cross, four times as wide as the required width. A centre fold and two folds, one either side, form a binding that will enclose a raw edge and accommodate curves.

Piping

Both piping and rouleau involve cutting fabric on the bias. The fabric is cut at 45° to the grain and most needlework shops or departments stock a bias cutter and folder. Any joins in the fabric must also be sewn on the bias before the cord is sewn in place. A bias strip of fabric cut from the same or a co-ordinating fabric as the embroidery, is first stitched to enclose a piping cord of the thickness required (diagram 11).

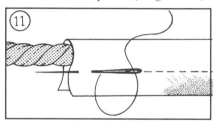

The handmade piping is a delightful finish for a piece of embroidery.

Rouleau

Bias-cut fabric is seamed, then turned inside out with a bodkin, blunt needle or a commercial rouleau turner (diagram 12). The rouleaux can then be used for ties to match a piece of embroidery.

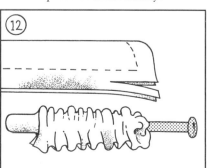

STITCHES

Left-handed workers should reverse any directions given with stitch instructions.

Back stitch   An even outline stitch which returns to the previous stitch before forming the new stitch (diagram 13).

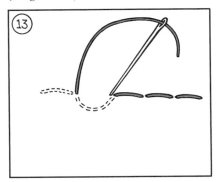

Buttonhole stitch   A stitch named for its original use. A looped stitch usually worked over a raw edge to prevent wear. Worked from left to right, the right-angled stitches are worked close together to form a looped edge (diagram 14a). A variation where the thread is wrapped around the needle each time is known as tailor's buttonhole stitch (diagram 14b).

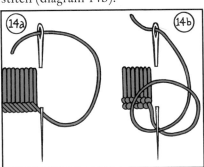

Chain stitch   A basic curved stitch named after the chain or tear shape formed by the loop through which each stitch is taken (diagram 15). Suitable for working in most threads, offering the worker a variety of smooth lines which will curve well. The stitch is worked from left to right.

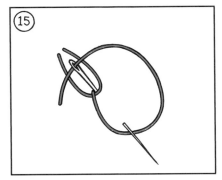

French knots   An essential stitch for all embroiderers, offering an effective seeding (diagram 16). Do persevere with this stitch which can prove daunting at first. The needle is reinserted close to the place at which it was brought through to the surface.

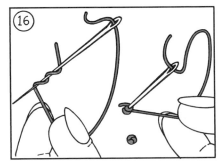

Herringbone stitch   A versatile stitch, equally useful as a practical hemming stitch and for decorative

effect. Worked from left to right, the two parallel rows of horizontal stitches are worked from top to bottom, right to left, bottom to top, right to left (diagram 17). This forms a line of overlapping diagonal stitches.

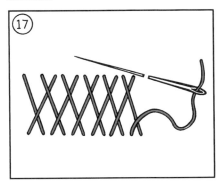

Picots   A small loop formed during the working of buttonhole stitch or oversewing. A pin is inserted in the fabric at right-angles to the stitching. As the stitching is worked, a loop is taken around the pin and then secured with a small stitch around the pin and pulled tightly (diagram 18). The pin is removed and the process repeated.

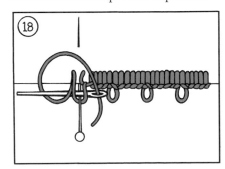

Pin stitch   A useful stitch, traditionally used for hemming on underwear and fine whitework. It has the dual advantage of forming a strong hem and creating a decorative finish with the same stitch. Worked from right to left, small punch holes are formed by the stitches. The horizontal and diagonal stitches form a continuous line of triangles which cover the fold of a hem or raw edge (diagram 19).

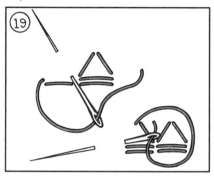

Running stitch   Useful as both a strengthening and decorative stitch, this is probably the simplest of stitches. Working from right to left, the needle is taken in and out of the fabric to form a broken straight line (diagram 20).

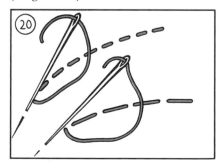

Satin stitch   Perhaps the most well-known stitch, attempted by most needleworkers (diagram 21).

Although overused in the past, the stitch is extremely effective, offering the worker shades of solid blocks of colour. The shade is achieved by different directions of stitches. Worked from left to right.

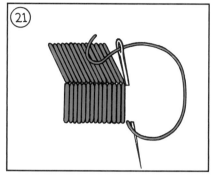

Slip stitch   A tiny stitch often used for a neat hem. The needle is slipped along and brought out to catch the two fabrics together almost invisibly (diagram 22).

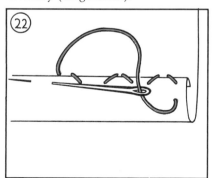

Split stitch   An alternative to stem stitch, this is useful for outlines. It is worked in a similar manner to stem stitch but as the needle is brought through to the surface, it splits the thread (diagram 23a). It can only be used with a soft, non-stranded thread.

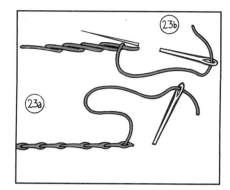

Stab stitch   An accurate version of running stitch, which is worked with the needle at right angles to the fabric, ensuring that the fabrics being stitched together do not move (diagram 24).

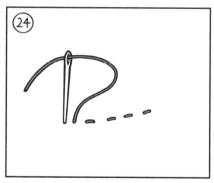

Stem stitch   A fine linear stitch, offering a rope like line (diagram 23b). The thickness can vary according to the thread used and the angle of the stitches.

Tacking stitch   A large variation of running stitch which is worked loosely to hold fabrics together temporarily. The large stitches are then easily removed when the permanent stitching is completed (diagram 20).

GLOSSARY

CARE

All the natural materials can be washed carefully by hand. Pure soapsuds are recommended, or saponaria root infusion for antique items (not saponaria leaves).

Gently immerse the work and allow the soiling to soak away through gentle movements in the water, then rinse all the washing agents away carefully.

Extra whiteness can be achieved by adding a capful of domestic bleach to a ten litre (two gallon) bucket of water and quickly immersing the item, then quickly and thoroughly rinsing.

A weak solution of traditional laundry starch will add a delightful crispness to cottons.

ACKNOWLEDGEMENTS

The authors would like to thank the following for their help with the book:

Helen Coxon, Kate Dew, Margeth Lingwood, John MacPherson, Rachel Selby, Dorothy Thomas, Sonja Turner, Susan Walker, Yan Watkins, Hazel Westwood and Stephanie Willis.

Acorn/Shade pull Attachment to cord on a roller blind.

Broderie anglaise/Eyelet lace (literally English embroidery) One of the most popular of the traditional whitework techniques.

Calico/Unbleached muslin Fabric used for dressing a tambour frame.

Card/Cardboard or Lightweight illustration board Used for templates.

Coton à broder/Brilliant embroidery cotton A highly-twisted, fine cotton embroidery thread.

Cotton bud/Q-tip or Cotton swab Used for removing spots of poster paint after a design has been worked.

Grain line A line following the warp threads, i.e. parallel to the selvage of the fabric.

Oversewing/Overcasting An embroidery stitch used in *Broderie anglaise*.

Perlé cotton/Pearl cotton A twisted embroidery thread with a lustrous sheen.

Piping/Cording A decorative edging made with *piping cord* and fabric.

Piping cord/Filler cord Strong cord available in various diameters, which is encased in fabric to make a decorative edging.

Rouleau/Tubing Used to make decorative edging or ties.

Slate frame/Scroll frame Rectangular frame used when working large pieces of embroidery or needlepoint.

Soft embroidery cotton/Matte embroidery cotton A thick, matt-finish embroidery thread.

Stranded cotton/Embroidery floss A loosely-twisted, six strand embroidery thread which can be separated for fine work.

Tack, tacking/Baste, basting A large, temporary running stitch.

Tambour frame Round frame used for working small pieces.

Turnings/Seam or hem allowance An amount of fabric added to the finished size of an item, enabling a seam or hem to be sewn.

INDEX